W9-BPJ-656

THE
KINGS
COUNTY
DISTILLERY

GUIDE TO
URBAN
MOONSHINING

THE KINGS COUNTY DISTILLERY

GUIDE TO
URBAN MOONSHINING

X X X

HOW TO MAKE
AND
DRINK WHISKEY

X X X

BY COLIN SPOELMAN
AND DAVID HASKELL

· ABRAMS, NEW YORK

ABOUT THIS BOOK

Kings County Distillery is an idea that turned into a pastime that grew into a business, but mostly it is an extension of a college friendship. Distilling whiskey takes time and requires patience. We wouldn't have lasted very long at it if we didn't enjoy each other's company.

Kings County is predicated on a discovery: You can actually make very good whiskey at home, and reasonably easily, and the possibilities of whiskey are much greater than what liquor store shelves suggest. That seemed to us like an opportunity, something worth exploring in our time off.

This book is something of an attempt to answer the many questions we stumbled over as we taught ourselves to make whiskey. It is a collaborative effort, written by Colin and edited by David, and we hope it provokes other old friends to start making some of what they drink.

PROLOGUE 9

CHAPTER ONE
WHAT IS WHISKEY?
17

CHAPTER TWO
A HISTORY OF WHISKEY
33

CHAPTER THREE
A SURVEY OF WHISKEYS
67

CHAPTER FOUR
HOW TO MAKE WHISKEY
113

CHAPTER FIVE
HOW TO DRINK WHISKEY
157

RESOURCES 207
GLOSSARY 210
INDEX 216
ABOUT THE AUTHORS 221
ACKNOWLEDGMENTS 222
CREDITS 224

PROLOGUE

It's hard to find a drink in eastern Kentucky. When I was in high school, there were rumors of a Coke machine in the clubhouse at the nine-hole country club that spit out cans of free beer. There were stories you could get alcohol at the VFW, but nobody ever seemed to go there. Harlan County was dry, which meant that selling any intoxicating beverages was forbidden by laws as old as Prohibition. For most people, bootleggers proved to be the most convenient solution. They were closer than the drive to the nearest "wet" town, half an hour away, or to Virginia, which, while closer on the map, was over two mountains. Also, bootleggers didn't card.

Our bootlegger lived on Pine Mountain, in a gray trailer that sat in a gravel lot by the side of the road that could have been mistaken for a widening of the shoulder. The yard, or what there was of it, offered views out over the Cumberland River valley. I wasn't old enough to drive, but my friend Derek was, and he had the connection.

You turned off the main road into the little parking area between the house and a corrugated metal shed. You shut the headlights off (business here was done after dark). A man emerged from the rear of the house with a flashlight, which he kept aimed at the ground or into his palm. He sold Zima, Mad Dog, and Seagram's 7, and maybe other things, but I was a sophomore in high school in the mid-1990s, and my worldview was limited. You told him what you were looking for; he would disappear behind the shed, sometimes for quite a while, and finally return with a brown paper bag. "Y'all be good," he'd say and then disappear. Then we would turn the headlights back on and back out of the driveway.

We didn't drink very often, but when we did, we'd head up into the hills with chasers, jerky, and dip tobacco, park the cars around a patch of dirt, and light a bonfire out on the artificial prairie of an

The town of Harlan, in eastern Kentucky, had been dry until a few years ago. Alcohol is now permitted in restaurants; only one has applied for the license.

abandoned strip mine. We called this "camping." There were no bands, no cocktails, no cover charge, and it was all ages, pretty much all the time. You could see for miles across the tops of the mountains. No one lived anywhere nearby. It was about as far from any sort of culture as we could get.

My father, a Presbyterian minister, spoke of bootleggers with disdain, but he kept an intellectual distance from any personal judgment. For instance, I don't think he'd have been critical of the owner of a grocery store that happened to sell beer; if theological push came to shove, I don't think he'd consider bootlegging itself sinful. It was the flouting of the law, the servicing of something secret and illicit, that made bootleggers culpable. Still, the community had standards and expected their clergy to embrace prevailing ethical principles, and so I was raised to view bootleggers as ideologically corrupt as well as lawless.

Eastern Kentucky then was becoming less isolated, thanks to VCRs and cable television, but even to this day it's still the type of place where you're lucky after pushing "seek" on the radio to catch a station.

Geographically, the town of Harlan is cut off by mountains that make it a day's drive to a shopping mall of any size. Each time a friend got his driver's license, a new world opened up, circumscribed by the Dairy Queen parking lot, an abandoned water plant covered with kudzu, the loading dock of an old coal tipple, and the strings of mostly empty roads in the valleys that connected them.

Only after living outside of Appalachia did I come to understand how unusual it was to grow up in a place with no liquor stores, no bars, and by extension, no restaurants. (It turns out that if people can't drink, they don't bother to go out to eat.) This may seem like a small thing, but it essentially precludes any evening activity outside the house. Nearly all of the places to eat in Harlan are fast-food chains. "Going out" might mean going to Pizza Hut, the only sit-down place with waiters. Maybe it's not surprising that kids tended to find their way more readily into sketchy situations, such as ditching class to go drink bootlegged Zima down by the river.

Most of my friends were patrons of the Pine Mountain bootlegger, but Smitty, the guitar player in my high school band Nicotine Jimmy Dog, preferred Mag's, a more mainstream option located conveniently in town. Mag Bailey sold liquor out of her house for nearly eighty years, just a few hundred feet from the elementary school. She was rumored to have escaped various prosecutions by paying federal excise tax on her sales, thus protecting herself from the most severe criminal penalties should things have gone south. It was also said that she bought off the local officials with well-placed bribes and long-term investments—she reportedly paid the law school expenses for some of the town's attorneys. I'm not sure that all of this is true, or that it explains everything, but everybody knew Mag and what she was up to, and she'd been operating with impunity for decades.

Mag lived on a street named after her. She had a paved blacktop circle behind an outbuilding next to the house—a kind of drive-through window—and kept an elderly man in her employ to run the shop. Mag's was open during the daylight hours, and I remember driving there as a fifteen-year-old on a bright fall afternoon with Smitty and picking up

The former home of well-known bootlegger Mag Bailey in Harlan.
Alcohol was resold from the garage next to the house to patrons who drove
down the adjacent alley to a waiting area.

a pint of Southern Comfort before going to band practice. Mag's sold moonshine, too, but when you're not old enough to drive, you sort of want to start with something manageable.

Mag Bailey died in 2005 at the age of 101. Her passing was eulogized in the *Lexington Herald-Leader*, on the Jimmy Buffett fan website, and on NPR. Otis Doan, perhaps one of her commissioned lawyers, gave a folksy interview and filled in some token nostalgia about Mag's life and her old practices. Otis's son Sean was in my class at school and had the unusual habit of making bullying comments while he inhaled. Once I found Sean and another classmate pounding Budweisers in the bathroom at Creech Drugstore. They asked me if I wanted some and started inhaling the words "beer pressure" over and over again. These were the heady days of coming of age in a dry town, and to hear Otis Doan talking about Mag with such affinity prompted mixed feelings.

Five years after Mag died, the municipality of Harlan voted to go provisionally wet as part of a political compromise between the abstinent and pro-booze factions. Restaurants could serve alcohol if more than 70 percent of their sales came from food, though package sales would still be forbidden. The only restaurant slated to take advantage of this, El Charrito, famous for its *Pollo Harlan*, had explored opening a second location so as not to subject their teetotaling customers to the inevitable unruliness of a booze-sodden restaurant environment. Ken Moody, owner of a restaurant called the Western Sizzlin', said he wouldn't serve alcohol because he had "morals" (the business has since changed hands and the new owners are pursuing a license).

But the writing is already on the wall. The era of the bootlegger is dying. Around the country, blue laws restricting alcohol sales are relaxing. South Carolina, which used to mandate that spirits be served via miniature airplane bottles, retired that law in 2006 (though the tradition of putting red polka dots on liquor stores, once a way to flout a ban on signage, remains). Most states now allow liquor sales on Sunday. Washington recently privatized state-run liquor stores. In Utah, patrons no longer have to apply for membership to drink in bars, though alcohol in restaurants must still be hidden from view. Many states allow liquor sales in grocery stores. And just as it is becoming easier to buy and drink alcohol, prohibitive restrictions on making it are easing, which has prompted a gold rush of new distilleries.

"Craft distillery" has become the industry term for an independently owned, small distillery making no more than 100,000 gallons of spirit a year, though many produce far less (and some are no longer independently owned). According to Michael Kinstlick, who studied the boom in craft distilling for the American Distilling Institute, there were only six operating craft distilleries in the United States in 1990. By 2000, there were about 25. By 2012, more than 250 were operating in all but five states. That number is expected to climb to 1,000 in the next decade.

The Appalachian moonshiner, once working only by the light of the moon, now has his own reality television show. Another television show, set in a fictionalized Harlan County, had a plotline featuring a colorful bootlegger named Mags. And while I expect there are now far fewer Appalachian moonshine operations run for profit than there were a decade ago, there are hundreds of home distilleries popping up in cities, suburbs, and rural areas. A new generation of moonshiners is making whiskey not out of economic necessity or alcoholic scarcity, but out of affinity for the drink, or just curiosity. Websites with forums catering to amateur distillers have proliferated. Home-brew supply stores now sell distillers yeast and other items that could only be used for moonshining.

Mike Haney, who lives in Barlow, Kentucky, had a family history of moonshining. In early 2011, he posted a YouTube video of a reflux moonshine still he'd built himself out of copper that he called the Hillbilly Flute. He started receiving interest from other hobbyists and requests to build stills. That year, he started Hillbilly Stills. In the first year of operation, he built 20 stillheads. By his third year, he was building more than 170, had constructed a new 4,000-square-foot warehouse on the remainder of his property, and had hired nine employees to help ship stills to (mostly illegal) distillers around the country.

The same year that Mag died, I was back in Kentucky and got my hands on a gallon of moonshine from a bootlegger. I brought it back to Brooklyn and shared it with friends at parties. It was popular. As my supply started to run out, I said to David at his birthday party what I had been thinking for some time: Why don't we try to make it ourselves? Surely it couldn't be that hard. And it *isn't* terrifically hard to make some sort of distilled alcohol. After about a year of the two of us bootlegging and, yes, selling bottles on the sly, I started to get calls from people I didn't know who wanted to blog about the moonshine. Our sphere of influence had gotten larger than was comfortable. That's when David suggested we look into getting a license, only just then realizing what a fortuitous time it was for distilling, as newly relaxed laws made it easier than ever to start a commercial distillery in New York. Our plan was to keep doing what we were doing, at barely more than a hobbyist's scale, and thus make legal moonshine for friends and neighbors.

In April 2010, the first drops of whiskey legally distilled in New York City in nearly ninety years began to flow from an eight-gallon

A gallon of Kentucky moonshine, obtained in 2005 through
an intermediary from an unknown bootlegger.

stainless-steel still in a 325-square-foot room in Brooklyn, otherwise known as Kings County Distillery, then the smallest distillery in the country. We quickly outgrew that space and relocated to a larger home at the former Paymaster Building of the Brooklyn Navy Yard. And as we've expanded, we've watched New York City's distilling community grow with us. Since we received our license, ten additional distilleries have opened in the borough of Brooklyn and two in the Bronx, all of us helping to return New York City to a place of prominence in the distilling world, a position it had held throughout the first three centuries of its existence.

It's a good time to be a glass of whiskey in America.

"In like Manner, since our Imports of Spirit have become so precarious, nay impracticable, on Account of the Enemy's Fleet which infests our Whole Coast, I would beg leave to suggest the propriety of erecting Public Distilleries in different States. The benefits arising from moderate use of Liquor, have been experienced in All Armies, and are not to be disputed!"

—GEORGE WASHINGTON
to the President of Congress, 1777

CHAPTER ONE

WHAT
IS
WHISKEY?

Andy Atkins used to drink Elijah Craig. He drove to Richmond to get it, which was a full day's trip from Harlan, and in order to make the trip especially worthwhile, he would drink the entire bottle in one sitting. On these nights, Andy would inexplicably become "Julio." He would no longer answer to Andy. He became sort of charmingly obnoxious for a bit, jumping over the fire and bleating obscenities. I was impressed. Elijah Craig became the nicest drink I could imagine. The bottle even came in a commemorative box.

This was my introduction to bourbon, as a freshman in high school, and I can't say my education went too much further over the next eight years. I would often pick up a glass of whiskey, become disappointed with myself that I didn't seem to be getting something right, look longingly at a beer, and try to make peace with my lack of refinement. I would think back, with comfort, to the woods of Kentucky, where everyone seemed to assume that the contents of the bottle were there simply for getting drunk. And I suppose this is how all drinkers begin, in the woods with a drunk named Julio roaring into the darkness against the crickets and the owls.

But then you grow up and are asked to know things. And at a certain point, that includes things about drinking—not just because there are expectations of maturity, but also because of the great void of the bar, which is something you must contend with again and again if you are a drinking adult living anywhere other than the woods of a dry county in Kentucky. So there you are, sitting on a stool, and the person behind the bar is going to ask you a question and you have to answer it. The answer is basically arbitrary. Most surely the answer will be ethanol, CH_3CH_2OH, but of course you don't say that. You feel that saying spiced rum, a gin rickey, or Johnnie Walker Blue Label will make your presence in the liquid pharmacy a little less arbitrary. You may have found you can get away with knowing nothing about wine, that you can call mulligan on that one and still get by. But liquor feels

Unlike the corn that you eat, corn grown for whiskey is dried on the stalk late into the season. This is Lakeview Organic Grain's farm in Penn Yan, New York.

different, and so you pick one drink to order everywhere you go, like you're James Bond or a cowboy. And you look down the bar and your ten-year-old self is sitting there shaking his head at how much of a phony you've become, and you want to say to him, *You don't understand; it gets complicated.* You want to explain that adulthood is something of an insult that prompts the whiskey in the first place. Who knew that you had to live with yourself in your own head for such a long time? Alcohol seems to soften the intensity of that fact. Great writers have articulated this same truth, and have dealt with the condition by turning to drink. So you look at your younger self and shrug. He'll understand soon enough. And who let him in the bar anyway?

You settle on whiskey, and you would be right to do that. And you know that there is whiskey and there is bourbon and there is scotch, all of which seem to be different somehow. You may have heard that bourbon must be made in Kentucky and something about Bourbon County. You have heard that water makes a difference, as does age. There is something called sour mash, which seems to be a good thing. But that's about it. Few seem to be much help on the topic—even the bartender isn't sure. In fact, there hasn't been much information available to you or anyone else: The sales reps and advertising copy for liquor brands say very little of any substance. The problem is that, for the last eighty years, the act of drinking whiskey has been drastically distanced from the act of making it. And since home distilling, which is arguably the best way to learn about spirits, is illegal, there aren't that many people who know how to talk with any authority about distillation.

When home brewing became legal in 1978, a renewed interest in beer led to more-knowledgeable consumers, the establishment of craft breweries, and far more variety in bar and store offerings. Although laws around distilling may not be relaxed in the near future, the arrival of small distilleries may begin to resolve this disconnect common among drinkers: How can you know so little about something you do so often?

x x x

In the old days, it was easy: Whiskey was distilled beer, and brandy was distilled wine. That was pretty much the entire survey of distilled spirits until the 1600s, when rum was invented, and from that point on, the landscape of distilled spirits got more complex. Whiskey itself became subdivided into many categories. For American whiskey, those categories refer to the primary grain ingredient—corn for bourbon, rye for rye, malted barley for malt whiskey, etc. Other whiskeys are usually classified by the country from which they originate: Scotch whisky and Canadian whisky (both spelled without the "e"), as well as Japanese and Irish whiskey, each have their own rules, including ones that restrict their production to their home country. So all bourbon is whiskey, but not all whiskey is bourbon. Same for scotch, rye, and other subcategories— they are all types of whiskey.

Contrary to myth, you can make bourbon anywhere in the United States, and indeed small distillers are making bourbon in

Colorado, Wisconsin, New York, and even Texas. As a Kentuckian, I used to insist that bourbon must be made in Kentucky, but that isn't true. (For a short while after I learned this truth, I continued to perpetuate the false perception out of state loyalty.) One aspect of the myth is true, though: You can't mislead the consumer as to where it is made, so only Kentucky bourbon is made in Kentucky. Sometimes distilleries will make bourbon but prefer to call it something else. For instance, Jack Daniel's is described as Tennessee whiskey, even though it could also be called bourbon. Some Tennessee whiskeys use a charcoal filtering method, known as the Lincoln County Process, but since not all of them do, the only thing that really makes Tennessee whiskey distinctive is geography.

Let's get more specific. To say that whiskey is distilled beer is accurate, but to be precise, whiskey is a spirit made from a fermented grain mash, distilled to a low proof, and usually, but not always, aged in barrels. A fermented grain mash—that is, a beer-like liquid at around 5 to 8 percent alcohol—can be made with corn, rice, oats, wheat, spelt, or quinoa. It cannot be made with sugar, fruit, agave, or honey. Not all fermented grain mashes become whiskey, however. Which brings us to the second part of the definition of whiskey, that bit about low-proof distillation.

Historically, whiskey was made in crude stills, known as pot stills or alembics. A pot still is capable of separating alcohol from the rest of the mash, but the spirit will retain a fair number of impurities that give whiskey and other flavorful spirits (like brandy) their distinctive taste. The spirit that results from a single distillation is so impure it is undrinkable; whiskey distilleries using pot stills must redistill their spirit at least once to remove the most unpalatable impurities. Theoretically, whiskey distilleries could continue to redistill further, each time increasing the alcohol percentage and removing further impurities and flavor. Eventually, this spirit would approach pure, tasteless ethanol. But making such a high-proof spirit on a pot still is extremely labor intensive and impractical.

In the early 1800s, Anneas Coffey invented a still that could distill to a much higher proof than regular pot distillation. This type of

A fermenting whiskey corn mash, with yeast actively converting sugar into alcohol.

distillation, known as column, reflux, or fractional distillation, forces many distillations within the still itself, and yields a pure spirit that is more neutral to the palate. This higher proof spirit, known in the United States as neutral grain spirit (NGS), is also called grain whisky in Scotland. Another common name for the spirit made from high-proof stills: vodka. Vodka is described by United States law as spirits distilled at 95 percent alcohol or higher, and having no distinctive character. Whiskey and most vodka are both made with grain, but the distinction is in how they are distilled and whether the objective is to retain or remove flavor.

Many commercial whiskey distilleries in America now use reflux stills, which can be calibrated to mimic pot stills during whiskey distillation and are more efficient. But Scottish law mandates pot stills for whiskey production, and many distillers believe the best whiskey is made from these cruder stills. Most American and Scotch whiskeys are distilled twice, whereas Irish whiskey is distilled three times. Jameson would have you believe that the third distillation enhances the quality

At Kings County, four small pot stills distill one hundred gallons of mash into twenty gallons of low wines, which are then redistilled by a fifth still into high-proof white whiskey.

of their whiskey, but it simply means that Jameson is more neutral: fewer impurities, less flavor.

The final component to most whiskey is aging, which plays probably the biggest role in how a whiskey looks and tastes. Any spirit that is unaged will be clear (gin, silver tequila, grappa, vodka, some rum), and any spirit that has aged will be yellow or brown (dark rum, brandy, whiskey, and reposado and añejo tequilas). There is one exception where a whiskey can be unaged: Corn whiskey is the only American category of whiskey that is legally allowed to be sold unaged. But all other American whiskey must, by law, sit in a barrel. Jack Daniel's recently tried to release a product called "unaged rye whiskey," but the federal government forced them to change their label to read "Tennessee Rye Spirits Distilled from Grain," which is inelegant, if not confusing. The federal government doesn't specify how *long* whiskey has to age, however. Some distillers will rest their spirit in an oak barrel for just a few minutes and call it whiskey.

Since the 1870s, unaged whiskey has held a second-class position among whiskeys. Commercial distilleries chose to age their product to improve it and distinguish it by sight from illegally made clear whiskey, known as moonshine, or cheaply made commercial whiskey. The word *moonshine* today can refer to any illegally made alcohol, but historically referred to unaged spirits made from corn. I use moonshine as a synonym for unaged whiskey, which I realize is controversial; some purists argue that moonshine refers only to illegally made spirits. But until other terms for unaged whiskey—white whiskey, white dog, white lightning, or new make—enter the vernacular, moonshine is probably the best word we have.

Within each category of whiskey, there are, of course, subtle variations. Among American whiskeys, there are straight whiskeys (aged two years) and "bottled-in-bond," a more restrictive subset of straight whiskeys. Among bourbons, there are rye, high-rye, and wheated variations of the corn-dominant mash bill. And no matter the ingredients, bourbon can be made with either a conventional mash process or a sour mash, which recycles spent liquid after distillation into the next batch's new mash (somewhat like the process for making sourdough bread). Most commercial bourbons use a sour mash process; most craft distillers do not. There are five distinct types of Scotch whisky, though single malt and blended are the most common. Whiskey is made in at least eighteen countries, many of which are mimicking scotch-style whiskey, and we can assume the American small-distillery movement will expand beyond the United States in time. You can already pour a shot of whiskey a day for many years and never have to drink the same whiskey twice.

x x x

When asked by the bartender to order a drink, you would be right to order a whiskey, but you wouldn't be typical. Statistically, Americans are more likely to order vodka. (This country drank 63 million cases of vodka in 2011.) And among those average Americans, one out of every ten orders a "super-premium" vodka, like Grey Goose, Belvedere, Ciroc, or Ketel One. If you take anything from this book, I hope it will be that every vodka order is a missed opportunity.

Vodka is a feat of engineering. By definition via American law, it has no "distinctive character, aroma, taste, or color," and so vodkas differentiate themselves by the vague characteristic of smoothness. This is not purely marketing, but it is a narrow way to judge a spirit. Smoothness is achieved not by trial and error, or experimentation, or happenstance, or tradition, but by industrialized, scientifically rigorous, efficiency-optimized equipment. There are no ghosts in vodka. It is the least lyrical of spirits, made to be adulterated, covered over, diluted, and hidden.

If an invisible dose of ethanol is what you're looking for, then I suppose vodka makes sense. When I first moved to New York, my vaguely Russian roommate used to take me to the Russian Samovar, a restaurant a few blocks from Times Square, where we would order infused vodkas from a simple list. The type of vodka is not important at Samovar; it's merely the vehicle for the infusions that can be seen in glass infusion jars behind the bar. This strikes me as the right way to drink vodka: minimum pretense, and flavored after the fact with fruits, herbs, and roots to let the drink become something else.

It can be intense to drink distilled ethanol (which, incidentally, comprises 10 percent of commercial gasoline—don't think about that too hard) right from the still, so over time, distillers learned to dress up vodka in lots of different ways. Most gin and absinthe originate as vodka before being infused and redistilled with flavoring agents. Liqueurs such as triple-sec, schnapps, amaretto, and ouzo are vodkas infused through a process not unlike the Russian Samovar's, with sugar added. But vodka succeeds at being the most versatile spirit because it's the least interesting, which suggests that the astronomic sales of super-premium vodkas are one of the great advertising triumphs of modern history. Incidentally, this is true not only of big players like Grey Goose. I've seen several small distilleries bill their vodka as a sipping vodka, pointing out the positive aspects of the taste of their spirits. This is by

Barrels are best tested for maturity by taste. Kings County's master blender, Nicole Austin, samples a barrel of rye.

definition impossible. If they are making vodka that has a taste, they are breaking the law.

Why not drink something else? Gin is flavored vodka by a different name. Rum can be an interesting spirit, but too often reminds me of its origin as a cheap alternative to whiskey and brandy, made by slaveholding colonialists out to create something intoxicating the easiest way possible. Tequila and its cousin mezcal get closer to a true craftsman's spirit, but they can be made only in certain parts of Mexico. Brandy is, to my mind, the only other spirit competitive to whiskey as a rewarding quotidian drink, though for me it, too, sits at a far remove from American history and experience.

Whiskey, though—whiskey is steeped in America. It is the spirit that George Washington distilled at home and offered to his troops during the Revolutionary War, and the spirit Thomas Jefferson foresaw when granting land in western Virginia to corn growers. It is the spirit that defined the soul of the South after its defeat in the Civil War, and the spirit that was most easily manufactured (sometimes through grossly

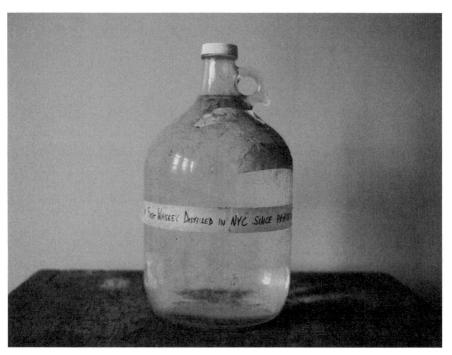

Whiskey is usually diluted before bottling with distilled water, though moonshine is sometimes sold at still strength for convenience. We saved Kings County's first legal whiskey run for posterity.

artificial means) during Prohibition, fueling the urban speakeasies of the Jazz Age, before the hangover of the Great Depression. And it is the spirit of Appalachian moonshiners throughout Prohibition's long and tangled aftermath.

Whiskey evokes the place of its making, as weather and climate influence its fermentation and aging. It measures time in degrees of color and taste, the liquid gradually darkening and mellowing in a warehouse full of wood ticking and creaking as shifts in temperature mediate pressure in the barrels through the seasons. It tastes of both past and present. It is, literally, a field of grain, cooked and fermented; distilled and aged; reduced to something of such great and abstract value that it is cherished next to art and literature. It is simultaneously inert and living, conservative and liberal, rarefied and common. Of all the spirits, it is the most challenging and rewarding to make, as well as the most personal. There is a reason why so many bourbons are named after people and so few other spirits are.

And so back to the metaphorical bar, and the question of what to drink. Let me offer some suggestions. Choose whiskey. Drink it neat. Try many kinds. Drink it outdoors if the weather permits, or near a fire if not. Drink it only on special occasions—though this is not meant to limit your consumption so much as force you to evaluate your blessings at any given time and consecrate them with whiskey. Whiskey is designed for company, and it is best shared. And the only proper way to consume it is to count your joys and acknowledge your sadness, and remind yourself of the ghosts of spirits past that live on in glass to glass.

WHAT AM I DRINKING?

The landscape of distilled spirits can be very confusing, but all liquors
can be classified based on four major variables: how it is aged, how it is
distilled, what it is made from, and where it is made. Unaged spirits are
clear and aged spirits are yellow to brown. Darker spirits are usually aged
in new barrels, from which they absorb more flavor, and lighter spirits are
usually aged in used barrels. In general, more flavorful spirits are distilled
in pot stills to a low proof, and more neutral spirits are distilled in column
stills to a higher proof. Grain, fruit, sugar, and agave are the most common
ingredients. And because countries have often protected the types of
spirits they produce, geography plays a role in what spirits may be called.

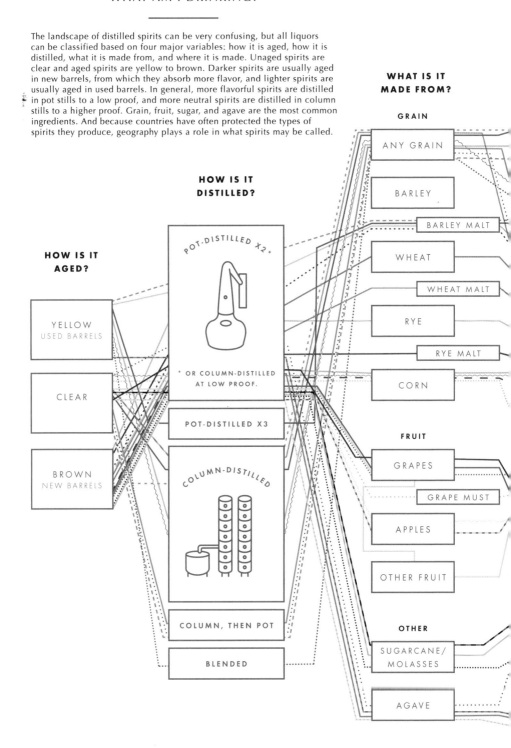

WHAT IS IT MADE FROM?

GRAIN

ANY GRAIN

BARLEY

BARLEY MALT

WHEAT

WHEAT MALT

RYE

RYE MALT

CORN

FRUIT

GRAPES

GRAPE MUST

APPLES

OTHER FRUIT

OTHER

SUGARCANE/ MOLASSES

AGAVE

HOW IS IT DISTILLED?

POT-DISTILLED X2 *

* OR COLUMN-DISTILLED AT LOW PROOF.

POT-DISTILLED X3

COLUMN-DISTILLED

COLUMN, THEN POT

BLENDED

HOW IS IT AGED?

YELLOW
USED BARRELS

CLEAR

BROWN
NEW BARRELS

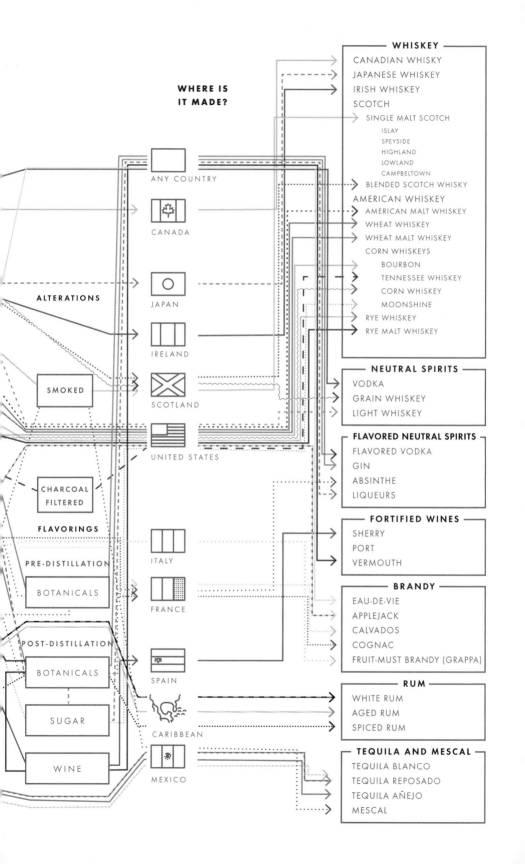

WHERE IS
IT MADE?

WHISKEY
CANADIAN WHISKY
JAPANESE WHISKEY
IRISH WHISKEY
SCOTCH
  SINGLE MALT SCOTCH
    ISLAY
    SPEYSIDE
    HIGHLAND
    LOWLAND
    CAMPBELTOWN
  BLENDED SCOTCH WHISKY
AMERICAN WHISKEY
  AMERICAN MALT WHISKEY
  WHEAT WHISKEY
  WHEAT MALT WHISKEY
  CORN WHISKEYS
    BOURBON
    TENNESSEE WHISKEY
    CORN WHISKEY
    MOONSHINE
  RYE WHISKEY
  RYE MALT WHISKEY

NEUTRAL SPIRITS
VODKA
GRAIN WHISKEY
LIGHT WHISKEY

FLAVORED NEUTRAL SPIRITS
FLAVORED VODKA
GIN
ABSINTHE
LIQUEURS

FORTIFIED WINES
SHERRY
PORT
VERMOUTH

BRANDY
EAU-DE-VIE
APPLEJACK
CALVADOS
COGNAC
FRUIT-MUST BRANDY (GRAPPA)

RUM
WHITE RUM
AGED RUM
SPICED RUM

TEQUILA AND MESCAL
TEQUILA BLANCO
TEQUILA REPOSADO
TEQUILA AÑEJO
MESCAL

ANY COUNTRY

CANADA

JAPAN

IRELAND

SCOTLAND

UNITED STATES

ITALY

FRANCE

SPAIN

CARIBBEAN

MEXICO

ALTERATIONS

SMOKED

CHARCOAL
FILTERED

FLAVORINGS

PRE-DISTILLATION

BOTANICALS

POST-DISTILLATION

BOTANICALS

SUGAR

WINE

"The Fifth Ward of Brooklyn is a section redolent of
fragrant memories. There it was that the 'moonshine'
industry flourished in all its glory. . . . The furtive
makers of 'Jersey lightning' who in recent times get
raided in their suburban retreats are simple amateurs
compared with their city prototypes. . . . They
had wild, barbaric ideas of what constituted real
'luxury'. An illustration was their big Investments in
costly jewelry. Nearly all of them wore 'headlight'
diamond studs, big as filberts and dazzling in their
luminous intensity. Now and again you would see a
boss distiller wearing a gold watch that weighed half
a pound, with a chain long and ponderous enough
to hang a ten-year old boy by the heels."

— "KINGS OF THE MOONSHINERS:
ILLICIT DISTILLERS WHO RULED IN 'IRISHTOWN,'"
NEW YORK TIMES, March 18, 1894

CHAPTER TWO

A
HISTORY
OF
WHISKEY

We tend to think of distilling as a rural phenomenon, something that happens in the rolling bluegrass hills of Kentucky near crystal clear streams where retired racehorses leisurely chew grass. But, in fact, the history of distilling in America is as much an urban story as it is a rural one, of northern states as well as southern states, of port cities as well as midwestern farmlands. Americans have prided themselves often on their moral integrity, which has placed liquor producers on the wrong end of the official record, and this has meant that the history of whiskey is cloudy at best. Still, it is certainly more significant, and colorful, than what is in textbooks.

Consider the Boston Molasses Flood of 1919, when a distillery operating on the waterfront lost a vat of ingredients. The tank ruptured, sending a fifteen-foot-high tidal wave of molasses through the streets, tearing buildings from their foundations and killing twenty-one people. Imagine a tidal wave of sugary liquid large enough to level a neighborhood, and you might get a sense of the scale of the urban distilling that used to go on in Boston and other large cities throughout the United States. And while distilling is starting to return to places outside of Kentucky, it's interesting to look back at whiskey's forgotten history for clues to understanding our own culture. Whiskey itself is liquid history, a reminder of the place and time of its making, and if one could drink a glass from every era in American whiskey history, their story might read something like this.

The first distillery in the United States was established by the Dutch on Staten Island, in present-day New York City, in 1640. It was described as a brandy distillery, though many historians agree that the still was producing whiskey, since it is unlikely that settlers would have found enough native fruit to support brandy production. When the British seized New Amsterdam in 1664, business leaders opened several distilleries to process the sugarcane and molasses arriving on ships from the Caribbean. Unlike the French and Spanish, who

Delancy's
Square

Fresh
Water

Th.° Jones Esq.[r]

Ship Yards

4   4   5

6   5   6

4

4   4

Brookland Ferry

J.Rapalie

3

Boundaries

5

3

3   Distillery
         Phil. Livingston Esq.[r]
         R.G.Livingston

BROOKLAND Parish

focused their explorations on finding fur or gold, the British intended to set up industry, and they did this through the rum trade. Throughout the seventeenth and eighteenth centuries, New York rum distilleries serviced not only the major cities of the northern colonies, but also the "triangular trade" that brought rum to Africa, slaves to the Caribbean, and sugarcane to the North. Rum also became a commodity for cross-Atlantic trade, creating an opportunity for supplies and travelers to cross the ocean and enriching the British colonies. A 1766 map illustrates very little development in Brooklyn, other than a large distillery complex in Brooklyn Heights standing among the scattered houses in the woods and marshes. King George III commissioned the map, and the fact that Livingston Distillery was the only industry highlighted may speak to the Crown's interests in distilling. By 1791, when records become available, the young United States was importing 7,194,606 gallons of molasses and producing 513,234 gallons of domestic spirit. The plan to develop American colonies via the liquor trade was so successful, in fact, that at a certain point, the residents of the British colonies felt like they no longer needed to pay for the support of the motherland, and fought the Revolutionary War to prove the point.

After the war, Alexander Hamilton, the first secretary of the treasury, was tasked with determining how the young government would pay for the limited services the new Constitution prescribed. The subject of taxes was a delicate one, with all that tea still steeping in the Boston Harbor, and so Hamilton proposed pinning a tax on spirits—a very American sleight of hand that shifted the debate from economic terms to moral ones.

However, one man's sin is another man's livelihood, and the farmers working small plots of land in the western frontier around Pittsburgh objected. These men weren't commercial distillers so much as yeomen moonshiners, tending to a copper pot over a fire, situated near small cornfields a long day's journey to town. Out on the frontier, it was considerably more difficult to deliver acres' worth of grain to market

The Ratzer Map of Brooklyn, this version drawn in 1766, identifies a distillery on the Livingston farm in what is now Brooklyn Heights. In the 1700s, distilling was an important colonial export; in the 1800s, it serviced a growing urban population.

A SELECTIVE TIMELINE OF WHISKEY HISTORY

While rum was the predominant distilled spirit of the British colonies in the 1700s, whiskey emerged as the American drink of choice soon after the Revolutionary War. American distillers spent much of the first half of the 1800s developing styles of whiskey—notably bourbon and rye—and much of the second half protesting, accommodating, and often skirting government regulation and taxation. Whiskey production practically ceased in 1920, with the arrival of Prohibition, and when it returned, it was quickly consolidated by a handful of large corporations. Since the turn of the millennium, American whiskey has undergone a resurgence, this time led by small craft distillers.

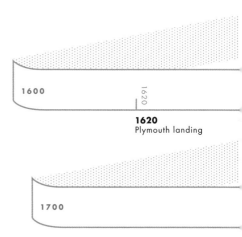

1600

1620

1620
Plymouth landing

1700

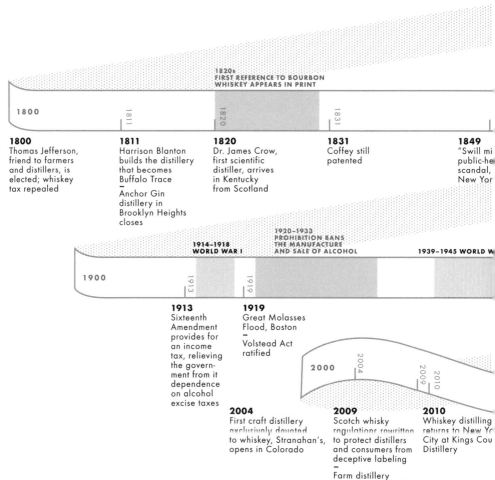

1820s
FIRST REFERENCE TO BOURBON
WHISKEY APPEARS IN PRINT

1800   1811   1820   1831   1849

1800
Thomas Jefferson, friend to farmers and distillers, is elected; whiskey tax repealed

1811
Harrison Blanton builds the distillery that becomes Buffalo Trace
–
Anchor Gin distillery in Brooklyn Heights closes

1820
Dr. James Crow, first scientific distiller, arrives in Kentucky from Scotland

1831
Coffey still patented

1849
"Swill mi public-he scandal, New Yor

1914–1918
WORLD WAR I

1920–1933
PROHIBITION BANS
THE MANUFACTURE
AND SALE OF ALCOHOL

1939–1945 WORLD W

1900   1913   1919

1913
Sixteenth Amendment provides for an income tax, relieving the govern-ment from it dependence on alcohol excise taxes

1919
Great Molasses Flood, Boston
–
Volstead Act ratified

2000   2004   2009   2010

2004
First craft distillery exclusively devoted to whiskey, Stranahan's, opens in Colorado

2009
Scotch whisky regulations rewritten to protect distillers and consumers from deceptive labeling
–
Farm distillery license introduced in New York State

2010
Whiskey distilling returns to New Yo City at Kings Cou Distillery

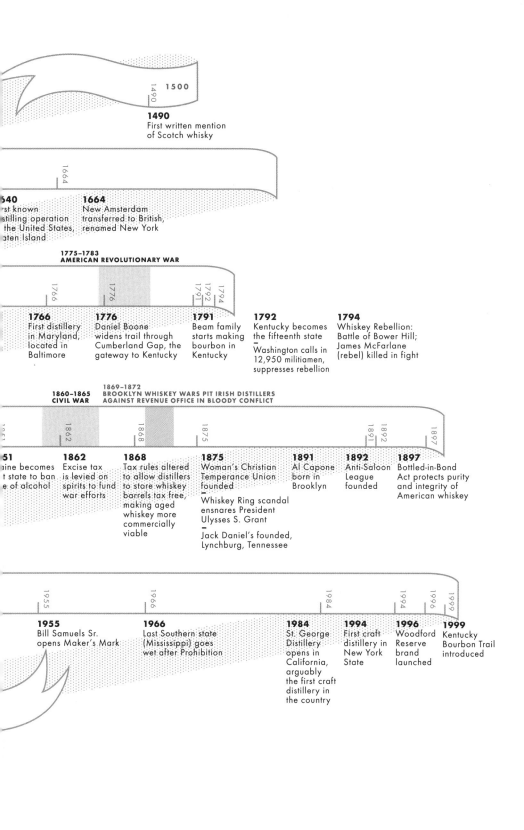

1500

1490
1490
First written mention
of Scotch whisky

1664

1664
New Amsterdam
transferred to British,
renamed New York

640
·st known
stilling operation
the United States,
aten Island

1775–1783
AMERICAN REVOLUTIONARY WAR

1766   1776   1792   1791   1794

1766
First distillery
in Maryland,
located in
Baltimore

1776
Daniel Boone
widens trail through
Cumberland Gap, the
gateway to Kentucky

1791
Beam family
starts making
bourbon in
Kentucky

1792
Kentucky becomes
the fifteenth state
–
Washington calls in
12,950 militiamen,
suppresses rebellion

1794
Whiskey Rebellion:
Battle of Bower Hill;
James McFarlane
(rebel) killed in fight

1860–1865
CIVIL WAR

1869–1872
BROOKLYN WHISKEY WARS PIT IRISH DISTILLERS
AGAINST REVENUE OFFICE IN BLOODY CONFLICT

1862   1868   1875   1891   1892   1897

51
·ine becomes
t state to ban
e of alcohol

1862
Excise tax
is levied on
spirits to fund
war efforts

1868
Tax rules altered
to allow distillers
to store whiskey
barrels tax free,
making aged
whiskey more
commercially
viable

1875
Woman's Christian
Temperance Union
founded
–
Whiskey Ring scandal
ensnares President
Ulysses S. Grant
–
Jack Daniel's founded,
Lynchburg, Tennessee

1891
Al Capone
born in
Brooklyn

1892
Anti-Saloon
League
founded

1897
Bottled-in-Bond
Act protects purity
and integrity of
American whiskey

1955   1966   1984   1994   1996   1999

1955
Bill Samuels Sr.
opens Maker's Mark

1966
Last Southern state
(Mississippi) goes
wet after Prohibition

1984
St. George
Distillery
opens in
California,
arguably
the first craft
distillery in
the country

1994
First craft
distillery in
New York
State

1996
Woodford
Reserve
brand
launched

1999
Kentucky
Bourbon Trail
introduced

During the Whiskey Rebellion, a crowd tars and feathers a tax collector in a public gesture of disgust with Alexander Hamilton's spirits tax.

than it was to distill the grain at home and travel with a jug of spirit. This is how whiskey first grew in popularity—it became a convenient mechanism for farms large and small to monetize their harvest. Then, as relations with the British began to sour, whiskey became the spirit of choice across the colonies: It was made and drunk locally, and not dependent on British influence or tastes.

These frontier farmers didn't think of their business as immoral. And furthermore, the rural farmers felt disproportionately penalized. Hamilton, a New Yorker, was surely aware that the large urban distilleries would have been able to afford the proposed excise tax, which was regressive and so decreased as production increased.

Hamilton's tax passed in 1791, and over the following years tensions between farmers and tax collectors grew. The farmers of Pennsylvania famously retaliated in a series of mostly nonviolent confrontations, which took place from 1791 to 1794, known to history as the Whiskey Rebellion. This mostly manifested itself in tax dodging and harassing tax collectors, but in the spring of 1794, a number of subpoenas were issued, and things got ugly. About 600 distillers and supportive militia banded together and laid siege to Bower Hill, the fortified home of General John Neville, a large-scale distiller turned tax collector, who was aiding the U.S. Marshal with a small group of soldiers. The siege lasted two days, and Neville went to hide in a nearby ravine. The rebels captured the marshal and commander of soldiers, which was seen as a victory, even though the hostages soon escaped.

After the successful raid on Bower Hill, the cause of the whiskey rebels became more generally the cause of poor farmers in western Pennsylvania, and talks of secession or attacking the wealthy town of Pittsburgh caused President George Washington to send in nearly 13,000 troops, an enormous show of force (the population of New York at the time was only 33,000).

With the arrival of Washington's troops, the rebellion dematerialized and federal hegemony was established. But the federal government's ambivalent relationship to whiskey can be seen in that early conflict: its moral disapproval, its dependence on excise tax revenue, and its consequent suspicion of outlaw distillers and tax evaders. Over the following centuries, the federal government kept the whiskey distiller in its sights, holding it back with one hand and picking its pocket with the other.

As for the frontier farmers of the young Republic, their complaints were assuaged (temporarily at least) by the election of Thomas Jefferson, who ran for president in 1800 on a platform of abolishing the excise tax. Like George Washington, whose Mount Vernon distillery made as much as 11,000 gallons a year, Jefferson knew the economic potential of whiskey. When he was governor of Virginia, he offered sixty-acre plots in the western part of his state to anyone who would grow corn. Sixty acres of corn was far more than any family could eat, but enough to support commercial distilling. In 1792, this part of Virginia became the fifteenth state: Kentucky.

x x x

During the next fifty years, settlers poured into Kentucky through the Cumberland Gap, which sits at the border of Kentucky, Tennessee, and Virginia. At first, they sent wagon trains of whiskey and herds of hogs back east on the same roads. But carting whiskey over the mountains proved difficult, and so distillers concentrated in the northern part of the state, where access to the Ohio River allowed whiskey makers a navigable trade route to the port city of New Orleans. In those days,

The Cumberland Gap was an early trade route that saw the constant traffic of settlers heading west, and hogs and whiskey barrels headed back east. Later, whiskey would be sent north to the Ohio River, destined for all points downriver, especially New Orleans.

whiskey was often unaged, but drinkers in New Orleans found that of the whiskey that *did* sit in barrels, that which came from the farthest away tasted the best (perhaps because it had been jostled the most and baked in the sun for the longest). These barrels were from the highest navigable point on the Ohio River, a flat area known as Limestone (today Maysville), where whiskey from much of eastern Kentucky landed to go to market. In 1786 there were six counties in the territory that would become Kentucky. The farthest east, and the highest up the river, was Bourbon County.

Within seven years, the county would assume its present-day boundaries, though the general area was still known as "Old Bourbon"—or at least its whiskey was described as being from there. Barrels with the word *bourbon* on the heads came to be prized in Francophile New Orleans (the county name honored the French for their help in the Revolutionary War, and the bourbon name may have suggested expensive aged French spirits, perhaps an early marketing strategy more than coincidence). Barrels were hard to come by in rural places, and old barrels were charred to sterilize the wood and remove bacteria, but this also had a mellowing effect on the whiskey inside, acting as a filter and infusing it with the caramelized sugars of the wood.

Today, many bourbon drinkers still claim that bourbon must come not just from Kentucky but from Bourbon County, but this makes no sense: There haven't been active distilleries in the smaller, present-day Bourbon County for at least a hundred years. There were many distilleries there in the early 1800s, and getting whiskey to market would have been an easy trip down the road still known as the Maysville Pike from Paris (formerly Bourbonton). Historians seem divided on whether bourbon gets its name from the larger territory, the present-day county, or something else entirely (one historian suggests the whiskey gets its name from Bourbon Street in New Orleans, and has nothing to do with Kentucky at all). In any case, most distillers moved west in the mid-1800s, and Kentucky's distillers are now concentrated in the western part of the state.

In the northeastern states, whiskey was made primarily from rye or a mixture of rye and corn. It was distilled in small batches in the rural counties, and at increasingly industrial scales in major cities. Baltimore had a distillery as early as 1761, built by Samuel Purviance of Philadelphia, and Maryland rye existed as a recognized type of whiskey up through the 1940s. Pennsylvania had as many as 5,000 stills making spirits by 1791. Many of today's small towns along Connecticut's shore had distilleries before 1800. Virginia had 3,600 stills operating as of the 1810 census, and whiskey making had a place alongside other spirits production. Swedish immigrants to Delaware made a persimmon brandy. In Brooklyn, the old Livingston Distillery, once surrounded by farms on the 1766 map, became the country's first gin distillery, owned until 1819 by Hezekiah Pierrepont, a major waterfront landowner. Pierrepont's great-grandfather founded Yale, and his second cousin twice removed, John Pierpont Morgan, would become an industrialist and banker synonymous with the American finance industry.

Urban distilleries benefitted from the influx of Irish immigrants, who knew a thing or two about making, and drinking, whiskey. Between 1840 and 1860, the population of New York more

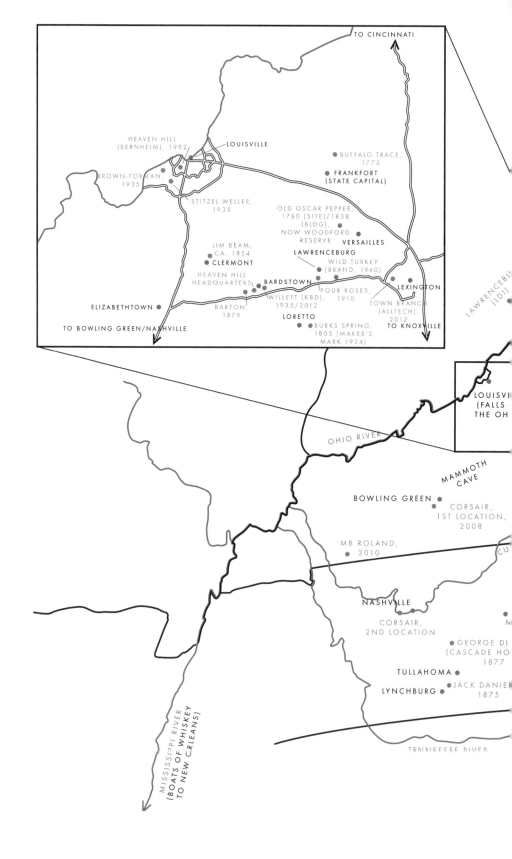

TO CINCINNATI

HEAVEN HILL
(BERNHEIM), 1992
LOUISVILLE

BUFFALO TRACE,
1773

BROWN-FORMAN,
1935

FRANKFORT
(STATE CAPITAL)

STITZEL-WELLER,
1935

OLD OSCAR PEPPER,
1780 (SITE)/1838
(BLDG),
NOW WOODFORD
RESERVE   VERSAILLES

JIM BEAM,
CA. 1854
CLERMONT

LAWRENCEBURG

WILD TURKEY
(BRAND, 1940)

HEAVEN HILL
HEADQUARTERS

BARDSTOWN

FOUR ROSES,
1910

LEXINGTON

WILLETT (KBD),
1935/2012

TOWN BRANCH
(ALLTECH),
2012

ELIZABETHTOWN

BARTON,
1879

LORETTO

TO KNOXVILLE

TO BOWLING GREEN/NASHVILLE

BURKS SPRING,
1805 (MAKER'S
MARK 1954)

LOUISVI
(FALLS
THE OH

OHIO RIVER

MAMMOTH
CAVE

LAWRENCEBU
(LDI)

BOWLING GREEN

CORSAIR,
1ST LOCATION,
2008

MB ROLAND,
2010

CU

NASHVILLE

CORSAIR,
2ND LOCATION

GEORGE DI
(CASCADE HO
1877

TULLAHOMA

LYNCHBURG

JACK DANIE
1875

M

MISSISSIPPI RIVER
(BOATS OF WHISKEY
TO NEW ORLEANS)

TENNESSEE RIVER

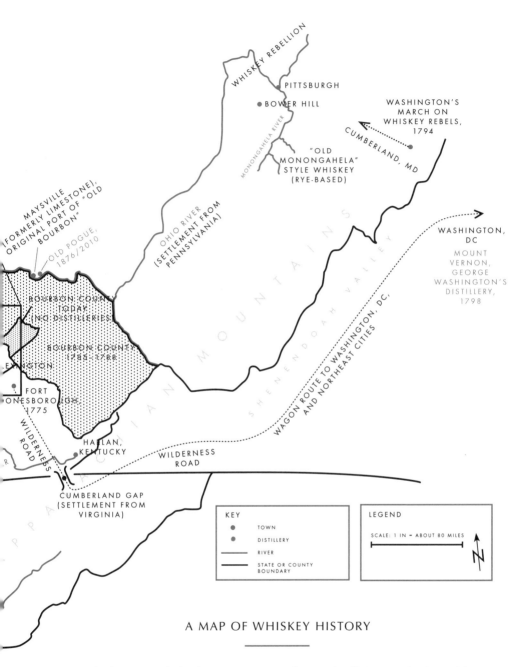

A MAP OF WHISKEY HISTORY

Much of America's whiskey history is concentrated geographically in Pennsylvania, Virginia, Tennessee, and Kentucky, or roughly the land area between the Tennessee and Ohio Rivers and their tributaries. In the early 1800s, as settlers moved into the Appalachian Mountains, down the Ohio River, and through the Cumberland Gap, farmers looking to convert commercial crops into a commodity established themselves as distillers. In the later part of the 1800s, these distillers moved further west, from the mountains into the knobby, rolling landscape of the Bluegrass Region, roughly between Lexington and Louisville. This map charts the major distilleries and when distilling began on those sites, as well as some of the important small distilleries currently operating, though many more could be included.

than doubled, as 500,000 new residents poured into the city. It was a time of remarkable alcohol consumption. Daniel Okrent, in his book *Last Call: The Rise and Fall of Prohibition*, found that in the 1830s, the equivalent of 1.7 bottles of liquor per person per week were consumed—and that's taking into account those who abstained from drinking (women most likely and children, we hope). One report from 1860 identifies a Brooklyn distillery, Johnson's, that produced 5 million gallons of whiskey annually. The population of New York at that time was 900,000, which means that a single distillery—and there were dozens of others—was producing about 5.5 gallons of whiskey per New Yorker each year.

Distillery news was frequently written up in the press. There were reports of fires, accidents, and in some papers, the scourge of "swill milk." Distilleries consume an enormous amount of grain, much of which remains intact after the distilling process, and many distilleries in both rural and urban areas kept dairy cows on the premises (and sold whiskey out the front and milk out the back, or vice versa depending on your proclivities). George Washington's distillery at Mount Vernon, for instance, supported 150 pigs and 30 cows. Pigs are better equipped to digest spent grain, but milk was especially needed in the cities. This might have been a symbiotic, sustainable arrangement, but cows are not built to be fed primarily on grain; and these particular New York cows were living in narrow, fetid quarters in the warehouse district near the waterfront. They frequently got sick and passed their diseases along through their milk, prompting a spike in the city's infant mortality rate. Temperance advocates made the obvious connection: Drink whiskey, and you are killing babies. Though that argument was made loudly and repeatedly in the press, it did very little to curb the city's thirst.

In 1862, when the outcome of the Civil War looked particularly bleak for the Union, Congress reinstated the excise tax. It was first pitched as an emergency wartime measure, though in the subsequent 150 years, it has never been repealed. Since 1862, any spirits made in the United States are subject to tax. A gallon of whiskey in 1865 cost $2.25 retail, $2 of which went to the government; a gallon

Many distilleries kept cattle, which were fed the spent stillage. Especially in cities, these distillery cows would often get sick and pass diseases on to infants and children who relied on their "swill milk."

of whiskey in 2013 must cost at least $13.50, which is the current rate of excise tax on 100-proof whiskey. An additional consequence of the return of the excise tax is that for more than 150 years, it has been illegal to own a still without obtaining a license from the federal government. Anyone making spirits in the United States is either abiding by strict measures enforced by the federal government or a law-breaking moonshiner.

The arrival of the excise tax immediately transformed the landscape of American distilling. Distilleries throughout the South were abandoned so that grain could be used for more practical purposes during the war. In the North, many distillers kept operating and simply flouted the tax laws. For instance, the Fifth Ward of Brooklyn, comprising what was then called Irishtown, was home to several commercial distilleries, and likely dozens of informal ones, run by immigrants who had brought from the Old World some knowledge of distilling, as well as a disdain for authority and a tradition of evading taxes. The neighborhood, situated between Fulton's ferry landing and the Navy

Yard, was particularly boisterous, lawless, and corrupt. It was the part of Brooklyn where sailors, dockworkers, and warehousemen went out for a good time, which usually involved some form of moonshine made on illegal stills, whether it was rum distilled from sugar refined on the waterfront or *poteen*, a high-proof clear spirit made from grain or potatoes. No one was paying federal taxes.

After the Civil War ended, Washington officials proposed that the excise tax become permanent, thus angering distillers around the country. The federal government, deeply in debt, went to great lengths to crack down on illegal stills, and enlisted returning soldiers to march alongside tax inspectors as military backup. Reinforcements were necessary: According to one report, the city of Brooklyn collected only $21,618 from distillers in 1867 even though it was estimated that the excise should have totaled $1,225,000 based on the volume consumed. The fact that many distilleries were owned by Northerners sympathetic to the Southern cause created a potentially explosive situation.

By the fall of 1869, Brooklyn's flagrancy had become too much for the federal government to ignore. With a Republican president back in office (the war hero Ulysses S. Grant), the administration's revenue arm sensed an opportunity. The federal inspectors in New York targeted the illegal moonshiners of Irishtown, and, as the weather grew cooler, they plotted their first raid.

A team of deputies converged on Dickson's Alley in the southeastern corner of the block currently bounded by York, Sands, and Navy streets (about 400 feet from where Kings County Distillery stands today). The deputies and revenue officers started by tearing down fences and breaking into outbuildings. Locals arrived on the scene to witness the excitement, and some sympathetic to the distillers began throwing stones. The raid was barely noted in the press, and did little to curb illegal moonshining. Revenue officials, however, determined that the provocative move would pay off if followed up with more might.

On December 4, a much more substantial raid was organized. Alfred Pleasanton, an ambitious yet somewhat inept former general with the Union army (he was a cavalry commander during the Battle of Gettysburg, which occurred in the first place because of the weakness of the cavalry's reconnaissance), served as the chief revenue collector. Pleasanton and about sixty revenue officers boarded the U.S.S. *Catalpa* at 5 A.M. in Manhattan to cross over to the Brooklyn Navy Yard, where they were joined by about a thousand troops. Axes and crowbars were handed out to the revenue officers, and a column of troops was assembled, marching out the western gate of the Navy Yard into the heart of Irishtown.

Throughout the snowy morning, the troops assisted the revenue officers as they broke up stills and disgorged the contents of the moonshiners' whiskey and rum barrels into the streets. As the *New York Times* reported:

> From the centre of a large wooden shed was tumbled out the largest and best apparatus yet seized. It was smoking hot, appeared to have been in full blast very recently, and was worth at least $2,000. Under this still in gigantic casks were thousands of gallons of dirty liquid, showing that the trade which was carried on here was not insignificant by any means. Buildings were ripped up, and tumbled down, floors were raised to find beneath more evidence and apparatus of the trade, and while all this was proceeding many curses, both loud and deep, were showered on the curse-proof heads of the deputies. Men who lived within the square [investigated] by the authorities were soon speaking in groups of twos, threes, and dozens, and with lowering looks and clenched teeth and fists, seemed to talk about sometime being able to destroy the enemy in detail.

As the army finished its work around noon, the crowd grew increasingly unruly and emboldened, lining the streets on their route back to the Navy Yard. At the corner of Plymouth and Hudson, rocks and bricks

hailed down at the revenue officers and, at one point, the army was forced to draw their guns on the crowd, scattering the gathered men. The *Times* summed up the affair:

> The number of stills seized is thirteen, and as it is understood that there are more illicit stills in the same region, it is not improbable that the "good work" will be protracted until they are all unearthed. The quantity of whisky poured on the streets in its pure state will sure go a great way toward disinfecting the Fifth Ward, even if it fails in reducing its rate of mortality. The general opinion relative to the streams of whiskey is, that pouring it out is the quickest way to settle disputes.

The *Brooklyn Eagle*, sympathetic to the Democrats (and the Irish), reported less on the activities of the army than on the indignation of the men who were mourning the lost whiskey, reprinting a speech by one Dennis Muldoon that criticized the troops as thieves preying exclusively on the poor.

On October 18, 1870, a revenue assessor and fifteen deputies again raided Dickson's Alley and broke up several stills. On their way back toward the Navy Yard, the deputies were fired on by the moonshiners. This worried the revenue commission enough to bring out the troops in serious numbers again, and now 1,500 soldiers were called up. According to one historian, there were more troops in Irishtown than were stationed in any Southern state to enforce reconstruction policy. The two-day raid netted twenty "distilleries."

In January 1871, the raids seemed to be losing their energy. "A score of troopers" were found drunk, and police and firemen refused to cooperate in pumping out the mash tubs. Many New Yorkers began to protest the conspicuous lack of arrests after so much display of military might. Many believed the police to be complicit with the moonshiners, and it became clear that without arrests, the stills of Irishtown would be

By 1900, nostalgia for moonshiners was already entering American culture. This image, depicting a moonshine operation in the woods of northern Georgia, ran in *Metropolitan Magazine* in 1906, ostensibly as an exposé but in fact glorifying the moonshine trade.

rebuilt and reassembled no matter how many raids were carried out. Finally, it was determined that men would be arrested and an example would be made visible for the entire community to witness. The stage was set for a showdown.

That summer, a smaller force of thirty-two revenue officers and soldiers from the Navy Yard set out to arrest four men: John Bridges, Michael Cassidy, James McMahon, and John Gorman. During the raid, Gorman escaped but Cassidy and McMahon were captured, despite the latter's attempt to evade arrest by jumping out of a third-story window. Gunfights broke out, and the shooting continued until a revenue officer, a spirits gauger named Clinton Gilbert, was fatally shot in the abdomen. The "whiskey wars," as they were dubbed in the press, had now turned deadly, and the tone of the conflict changed considerably. This was probably the first instance in American history of an IRS agent killed in the line of duty, though that number would climb to at least fifty-five by 1905, as revenue agents entered into trench warfare with moonshine distillers.

One historian argues that the whiskey wars of Brooklyn and other northern cities (Philadelphia saw its share of raids, too) were a part of a gradual shift in the public consciousness to accept a greater and more powerful federal government. They gave the North a taste of the reconstruction policies imposed on the South. But the other lasting effect of the whiskey wars is that distillers began to be viewed as lawless, immoral cheaters, and destructive to the community.

And also dangerous. From 1876 to 1905, federal records indicate seizures of some 30,763 illicit stills, and while city raids garnered major press, most were in the rural South. This was a time when the government received up to 65 percent of its revenue from excise tax and thus depended heavily on the income from spirits consumption. It hired hundreds of revenue agents to collect taxes and punish illegal distillers. In cities, moonshiners were constrained by their close proximity to public life, but rural moonshiners worked in secret—deep in the woods and protected with rifles and booby traps, such that if they ever were found, at least they wouldn't be caught. In the early years of the revenue agency, one in fifty raids resulted in the serious injury or death of revenue officers. The agency did not keep records of moonshiners killed.

As illicit moonshine boomed, so too did commercial whiskey. In 1868, the federal government amended the law to allow barreled whiskey to be stored in bonded warehouses, postponing tax assessments until the spirit left the distillery. This allowed distillers to age their products more deliberately and without tax consequences, and as a result American whiskey's flavor profile began to shift away from unaged and lightly aged whiskeys to something closer to the bourbon and rye commonly available today. Many accounts of the time begin to describe whiskey as having a reddish color, which would point to aging in newly charred barrels.

Before the late 1800s, whiskey was sold by the barrel to wholesalers, bars, and saloons that would dispense it in various containers or directly to the consumer. Some historians put George Garvin Brown, who would later become the Brown in Brown-Forman

Whiskey used to be bottled from the barrel by wholesalers. In the 1870s,
some brands began to bottle and seal at the distillery, giving customers
more protection from fraudulent bottles.

(the company that now owns Jack Daniel's, as well as many other spirits
brands), as the first distiller to begin to bottle his whiskey specifically
under a brand name (Old Forester), so as to ensure that consumers
knew what they were getting. Other distillers started to bottle whiskey
as patent medicines, increasing the market for what had previously
been sold only as an intoxicant.

But the halting steps toward building customer trust in one's
own brand of whiskey was the exception that proved the rule. In the
years between the Civil War and Prohibition, much of the whiskey being
produced would not have qualified as whiskey today. Often commercial
rectifiers would buy column-distilled spirits in bulk and use a number
of artificial treatments (like caramelized sugar, wood chips, beading
oil or glycerine, and prune juice) to mimic the color and flavor of true
whiskey. Only until the Bottled-in-Bond Act of 1897 did consumers
start to have government-sanctioned differentiation between legitimate
and adulterated whiskey. But even in 1917, only 16 million gallons of

The Whiskey Ring trial of 1875 exposed collusion among distillers and revenue agents to defraud the government of excise tax duties, a scandal that reached all the way to the White House, with Ulysses S. Grant's personal secretary indicted.

bottled-in-bond whiskey were made, compared to 115 million gallons of rectified spirits, much of which was sold as whiskey.

And corruption was everywhere. In an ironic footnote, President Grant, who for many years provided a target for the anger of moonshiners around the country, became embroiled in the controversy of the Whiskey Ring scandal of 1875, wherein distillers, distributors, spirits gaugers, and revenue officers were implicated in bilking the government out of its share of the spirits revenue through collusion and bribery. In the end, it seemed that both the Republicans and the Democrats were cheating on their liquor taxes, just in different ways.

By the turn of the century, both illegal moonshiners and established distilleries had eroded the public's trust, and the common view of distillers large and small was that they were detrimental to the fabric of society. Temperance was a progressive movement with a liberal agenda, a so-called noble experiment. Dry politicians and social activists argued that only a comprehensive ban on the sale and manufacture of alcohol would tame the rapacious capitalists and insolent lawbreakers.

A TREATISE

ON THE

MANUFACTURE, IMITATION, ADULTERATION, AND REDUCTION

OF

FOREIGN WINES,

BRANDIES, GINS, RUMS,

ETC. ETC.

INCLUDING

"OLD RYE" WHISKEY, "OLD RYE MONONGAHELA," "WHEAT," AND "BOURBON" WHISKEYS, FANCY BRANDIES, CORDIALS, AND DOMESTIC LIQUORS.

BASED UPON THE "FRENCH SYSTEM."

BY A PRACTICAL CHEMIST,

AND

EXPERIENCED LIQUOR DEALER.

John ___ Jackson

PHILADELPHIA:

PUBLISHED FOR THE AUTHOR.

1860.

In the later half of the 1800s, legitimate distillers had to contend with "imitation whiskies" made by spirits rectifiers who added sometimes-toxic additives to cheap, column-distilled neutral spirits. A book from 1860 offers recipes for imitation spirits.

It is easy now to look back at Prohibition and think of it as a backward moment, a stutter in the gradual progress of American history. But the culture of drinking in America had a very different tone before Prohibition. As Michael Lerner writes in his book *Dry Manhattan*:

> By 1913, according to the [Anti-Saloon] League, New Yorkers were spending $365 million a year on alcohol, a figure that translated neatly to the tune of a million dollars a day. This was more than double what the nation spent annually on the salaries of its public school teachers. In one week, the league claimed, New Yorkers consumed 30 million quarts of draft beer, a million quarts of bottled beer and ale, a half-million quarts of whiskey, 75,000 quarts of gin, 76,000 quarts of brandy, 500 quarts of absinthe, 40,500 quarts of champagne, 60,000 quarts of wine and nearly 500,000 quarts of other miscellaneous beers and liquors. Statewide, the league estimated that New Yorkers drank six quarts of alcoholic beverages a week.

While the league may have exaggerated their numbers somewhat, they are still pretty arresting. The enormous quantity of alcohol being consumed led to serious social problems: Men would spend a good portion of their earnings in bars, make poor business decisions, get in fights and accidents, and come home and be abusive to wives and children. America was simply much drunker, more of the time. Out of the temperance movement came many positive developments, such as an income tax and women's suffrage. But mostly, it gave the country a chance to dry out a bit after the bender that was the 1800s.

History moved quickly. In 1913, the passage of the Sixteenth Amendment provided for an income tax, which lowered the government's dependence on alcohol excise revenue. Six years later, Congress passed the Volstead Act, banning the manufacture and sale of alcohol. Prohibition went into effect on January 1, 1920.

x x x

Rural moonshiners often went to great lengths to avoid notice. This customized shoe has wooden cow hooves attached to the sole so as to disguise human footprints.

Prohibition, and the laws enacted following its repeal in 1933, changed much about the culture of alcohol. First, and perhaps most importantly, drinking socially became a co-ed activity; previously, women were rarely seen in saloons and taverns, but speakeasies were happy to cater to both sexes. After repeal, and in an effort to crack down on organized crime, the sale of alcohol remained heavily regulated, with laws separating entities that manufactured alcohol from those that sold to customers. Licensing fees for manufacturing alcohol were set high so that only major operations could afford them. As a result, few distilleries opened after Prohibition, and none in urban areas. A handful of Kentucky distilleries (including the distillery that is today called Buffalo Trace) had remained in business through the 1920s making medicinal whiskey, which allowed them something of a first-mover advantage. Most of the current Kentucky distilleries opened or reopened thereafter. The industry quickly consolidated, dying out completely in former places of prominence such as New York, Pennsylvania, and Maryland, and merging its Kentucky-area

STATEMENT SHOWING BY STATES AND TERRITORIES THE PRODUCTION OF DISTILLED
SPIRITS DURING THE YEARS 1916 AND 1917, COMPARED

States and territories	Fiscal year 1917			Total production, fiscal year 1916
	Spirits produced from materials other than fruit	Fruit brandy	Total production	
	Gallons	Gallons	Gallons	Gallons
Arkansas..........	....	....	....	178.4
California.........	9,979,723.4	7,871,759.0	17,851,482.4	11,845,251.1
Connecticut......	121,890.6	10,163.9	132,054.5	127,214.9
District of Columbia	608,812.2	....	608,812.2	1,664,389.3
Florida...........	....	....	....	2,715.1
Hawaii...........	14,015.5	....	14,015.5	13,671.9
Illinois...........	79,320,206.5	410.5	79,320,617.0	66,868,865.2
Indiana..........	43,332,771.0	28,504.9	43,361,275.9	51,108,395.3
Kentucky........	36,407,614.9	34,162.9	36,441,777.8	33,254,129.4
Louisiana	26,545,832.8	....	26,545,832.8	23,291,661.1
Maryland........	24,949,677.8	15,642.7	24,965,320.5	3,327,842.0
Massachusetts.....	12,511,179.8	58.5	12,511,238.3	11,609,189.1
Michigan.........	819,669.0	238.7	819,907.7	2,575,375.4
Missouri..........	283,972.8	5,687.7	289,660.5	194,171.9
Montana.........	244,772.5	....	244,772.5	52,385.8
Nebraska........	2,938,594.1	....	2,938,594.1	2,476,219.1
New Jersey......	....	54,493.8	54,493.8	56,158.3
New Mexico......	....	314.9	314.9	295.9
New York........	13,817,034.5	39,019.1	13,856,053.6	13,802,024.2
Ohio............	9,954,439.5	160,133.0	10,114,572.5	12,448,347.7
Pennsylvania......	12,177,573.5	13,190.1	12,190,763.6	14,408,130.3
Rhode Island.....	224.2	....	224.2	236.7
South Carolina....	1,159,308.5	....	1,159,308.5	1,179,890.0
Texas............	13,904.9	....	13,904.9	
Virginia..........	105,899.3	17,057.9	122,957.2	547,559.5
Washington.......	....	....	....	392.1
Wisconsin........	2,527,249.3	....	2,527,249.3	2,428,480.0
Wyoming........	....	259.7	259.7	103.0
Total.........	277,834,366.6	8,251,097.3	286,085,463.9	253,283,273.4

Though people often think of Kentucky and Tennessee as historic producers
of spirits, Illinois and Indiana were leading the country in production
by a large margin before Prohibition, as shown in this chart from a 1918 treatise.

distilleries such that almost all American whiskey was soon made by five large corporations.

When federal Prohibition ended in 1933, states were given the option to stay dry, and many did. In 1966, Mississippi became the last state to end statewide prohibition. Several states passed along the dry option to the county level, and today, hundreds of counties, primarily in the Southeast (and many in Kentucky), remain dry. After Prohibition, the moonshiner concentrated his trade in these areas, where running an illegal still was less an exercise in avoiding excise taxes than in providing an essential service.

Laws changing the way alcohol is sold have been gradually softening since 1933, but the laws restricting the way alcohol is made have experienced a more dramatic and sudden collapse, and this has occurred only in the last fifteen years. Starting on the West Coast, state governments have altered their spirits laws to make it less onerous for small businesses to acquire a license. This has led to hundreds of new distilleries opening just within the last decade—more than even the closest observers can count. California, New York, and Oregon are each now home to more than twenty.

Even in Kentucky, things are changing. The town of Maysville, which sits on the Ohio River and was once the port from which much of the whiskey barrels would have come downriver, has seen the reopening of a historic distillery—and so distilling has begun again in the boundaries of what was once called Bourbon County. Kentucky has a bourbon trail that is well known, but it has also launched a "craft tour" of smaller distilleries that are opening around the state. The historic Sitzel-Weller Distillery is opening again in Louisville. Big companies like Jim Beam and Jack Daniel's have released unaged whiskeys, acknowledging that people are interested in the full range of whiskeys, not just the now-ubiquitous four-year straight bourbons and ryes that represented only a fraction of the market before the Civil War.

Not that anyone imagines this distilling renaissance will substantially erode Kentucky's and Tennessee's prominence in the marketplace. Walking around downtown Brooklyn today, it's hard to picture the incredibly active distilling culture that once defined the neighborhood. The site of the former Livingston/Pierrepont Distillery is an expanse of concrete apron just under the Brooklyn-Queens Expressway. Newly converted lofts stand nearby, and the once sandy, cedar-covered bluffs are now lined with the stately homes of Brooklyn Heights. The wild tenements and illicit stills of Little Street in Irishtown have been replaced by a massive Con Edison substation, and most of Vinegar Hill is a ward of empty streets, surrounded only by the buzz of transformers and the whisper of the river. Dickson's Alley is buried under a tower of the Farragut Houses, a housing project just steps from the current location of Kings County Distillery. The Navy Yard has been decommissioned, and the officers' quarters, which once abutted Irishtown, are overgrown with trees and slated to become a supermarket. Al Capone—the greatest bootlegger of all time—was born a few steps from the Navy Yard, but today his birthplace is the site of an on-ramp to the BQE, and the brothels of Sands Street, where he contracted the syphilis that killed him, are gardens surrounded by public housing. All of this recent history has quickly covered over the past, the stench of alcohol having left only bitter memories in the public consciousness.

It's fun to imagine what distilling culture will look like in America in a hundred years. Perhaps home distillation will be decriminalized and every family will have a microstill next to the coffeepot, thus rendering commercial distilleries a fanciful relic of an industrial past. Or the country may be swept by a religious or social fervor that shrinks the culture of drinking yet again. Cultures change, landscapes change, buildings find new functions, and cities mature. Part of the pleasure of inhabiting them is imagining the ghosts that haunt the architectural remnants of other times, while thinking of our children's children and wondering if they'll ever bother to ask what came before. Certainly, a number of loyal Republican soldiers are turning in their graves as they watch Kings County Distillery's copper stills disgorging moonshine not in Irishtown, but inside the Navy Yard walls.

1. The Brooklyn Bridge
Begun in 1870 and finished in 1883, the Brooklyn Bridge opened up commerce between the island of Manhattan and its near neighbor, spurring development in Brooklyn.

2. Livingston/Pierrepont Distillery
The Livingston Distillery was on this site going back to at least 1766. It burned during the Revolutionary War and was acquired and enlarged later by Hezekiah Pierrepont, whose aged Anchor Gin was sold around the country. His wooden warehouses and windmill made the site a prominent landmark for visitors to Brooklyn by boat.

3. 42 Fuhrman Street
The Bache Sons & Co. distillery rectified grain spirits into gin, brandy, and vodka. Opened in 1811, it had a daily output of 3,800 gallons.

4. Cunningham & Harris Distillery
A distillery on this site offered spent mash fresh from the stills to anyone who would take it, via pipes and faucets that ran over the street. Farmers brought in wagons and filled up. But by 1845, Front Street had become frequently blocked by teamsters, who were in the habit of using coarse and obscene language; the city successfully sued, and the distillery was convicted of creating a public nuisance. (This was the same year that an 8-year-old boy was scalded to death, having fallen into a vat of spent mash.)

5. Sands Street
Sands Street was, until the 1950s, the main thoroughfare of this predominantly Irish neighborhood. The brothels, saloons, and gambling parlors along the street attracted a rough crowd, and violence was common here. Al Capone contracted syphilis at a brothel on this street in the early 1900s.

6. Johnson's Distillery
Another large distillery operated at the corner of Jay Street and Front Street, covering six lots and consuming 20,000 bushels of grain in a season.

7. Dickson's Alley
This small alley no longer exists, but it once ran for a few blocks between Front Street and Sands Street. Many illegal distillers concentrated here, and raids throughout the years from 1869 to 1872 targeted this block.

8. Hudson Avenue, Vinegar Hill
The wooden buildings that front Hudson Avenue are beautiful examples of nineteenth-century wooden architecture, a rarity in Brooklyn. Stop at Vinegar Hill House or its sister shop, Hillside, for a bite.

9. Little Street
Many illicit distillers concentrated in this area during and after the Civil War. Today, only a part of the street remains.

10. Commandant's House
This unusual mansion, built in 1805 just three years after the commissioning of the Navy Yard, is in private hands and remains one of the most mysterious and intriguing private residences in the city. It is rumored to have been designed by Charles Bulfinch, the architect of the U.S. Capitol's wings, rotunda, and portico.

11. 92 Navy Street
Birthplace of Al Capone.

12. Sands Street Gate
Revenue Officer Clinton Gilbert, killed in a moonshine raid in 1872, was told to seek safety here after being mortally wounded in the stomach.

13. Kings County Distillery
The first whiskey distillery in New York City since Prohibition occupies the Paymaster Building, built in 1899 as the financial administration building of the Navy Yard.

14. Building 92
The oldest building in the Navy Yard, designed in 1857 by Thomas U. Walter, who also designed the current cast-iron dome on the U.S. Capitol, is now used as a museum for the Navy Yard.

A WALKING TOUR OF WHISKEY HISTORY IN DOWNTOWN BROOKLYN

Brooklyn's history of distilling is easily accessed via a short walk along the waterfront from Brooklyn Heights to the Navy Yard, passing landmarks such as the Brooklyn Bridge, Grimaldi's Pizza, and Jane's Carousel. To begin the tour, take the subway to the Court Street N/R station or the Borough Hall 2/3 station. Or simply walk over the Brooklyn Bridge.

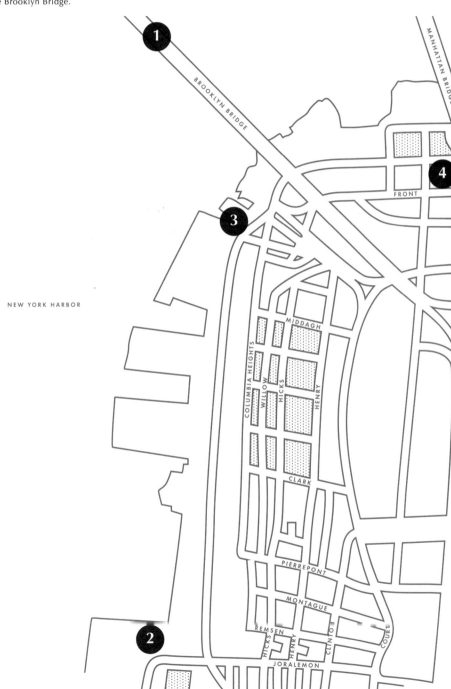

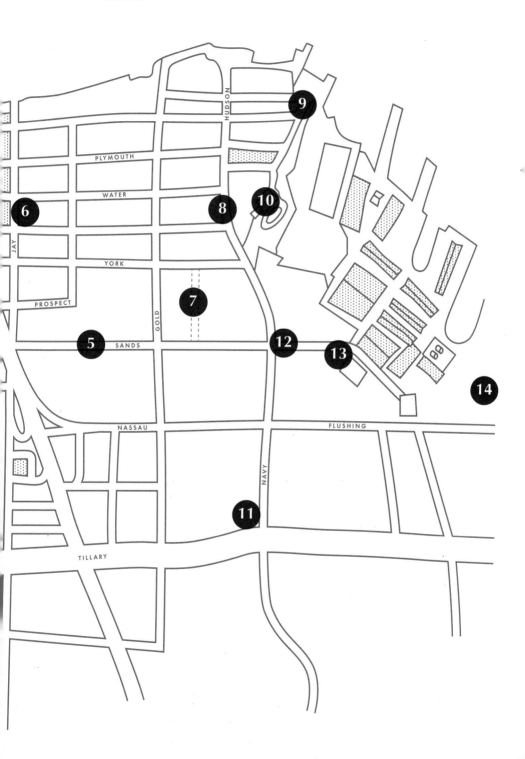

EAST RIVER

PLYMOUTH

WATER

HUDSON

YORK

PROSPECT

GOLD

SANDS

NASSAU

FLUSHING

NAVY

TILLARY

JAY

6

9

8

10

7

5

12

13

14

11

"I can hardly tell one bourbon from another, unless the other is very bad. Some bad bourbons are more memorable than good ones. For example, I can recall being broke with some friends in Tennessee and deciding to have a party and being able to afford only two-fifths of a $1.75 bourbon called Two Natural, whose label showed dice coming up 5 and 2. Its taste was memorable. The psychological effect was also notable. After knocking back two or three shots over a period of half an hour, the three male drinkers looked at each other and said in a single voice: 'Where are the women?' I have not been able to locate this remarkable bourbon since."

—WALKER PERCY

CHAPTER THREE

A
SURVEY
OF
WHISKEYS

PART 1

KENTUCKY WHISKEY

Lawrenceburg, Indiana, is a town just over the Ohio River from Kentucky, near Cincinnati. The distillery there is known colloquially as LDI (Lawrenceburg Distillers Indiana). It was once owned by Seagram's, but is now part of MGP, a food conglomerate that specializes in bioplastics, industrial proteins, and starches for use in salad dressings, energy bars, imitation cheese, and fruit fillings. The plant is a collection of nondescript brick buildings with the telltale small windows of barrel-storage rickhouses, situated along a muddy river known as Tanners Creek that dumps into the Ohio River a few hundred yards south. According to bourbon historian Michael Veach, distilling at this site goes back to 1807, and aerial images show the ruins of what was perhaps the Squibb Distillery, opened in the 1850s and rebuilt just before Prohibition. Today, LDI is pretty quiet. There is very little signage and only a few cars in its parking lot.

One of the products made in this facility is a rye whiskey with a mash bill of 95 percent rye, 5 percent malt. It is a strange mash bill. Most rye whiskeys are no more than 70 percent rye, just as bourbon is rarely more than 70 percent corn. According to author and blogger Chuck Cowdery, this particular whiskey was developed by Seagram's as a flavoring agent for blended whiskeys like Seagram's 7. When Seagram's disintegrated due to mismanagement in the 1990s, the whiskey, then in the process of aging, was sold to other distilleries in the fire sale of assets, as one salvage company after the next tried to determine what to do with the distillery and its excess inventory. This is how one generic whiskey became known by more than a dozen names, including Templeton Rye, Redemption Rye, Bulleit Rye, Willet, Smooth

The stillhouse of Jim Beam, where two column stills produce whiskey for Beam's brands.

Ambler, and George Dickel Rye, among others. The companies that own each of these brands have purchased LDI rye whiskey and now bottle it under their own labels, adjusting the proof and length of aging in order to create minor differentiations.

If it is surprising that about half of the rye brands on liquor shelves today are made in a single, industrial facility, it is even more startling that many of these brands are so-called craft distilleries. Of the remaining non-LDI ryes, only a handful are produced in the distilleries suggested by their label. While Jim Beam rye is indeed made at Jim Beam, Jefferson's Rye is made in Canada. A few craft distillers have aged ryes; one worth mentioning is Old Potrero, a side project of the Anchor Distilling Company that features one of the only American whiskeys aged in uncharred oak. But even WhistlePig, an ambitious starter in the craft field, sources whiskey for its bottles.

Rye is an easy target, perhaps, because the demand for rye whiskey is very high and the supply very low. It can be hard for craft distillers to make, as the grain gets gelatinous and can burn inside the still, mixing smoke in the vapor column and producing a foul-tasting distillate. Perhaps it is inevitable that certain shortcuts would be taken to satisfy the market. But it can be just as perplexing to look into bourbons, hoping for clarity on what it is, exactly, that you are drinking. Even sophisticated consumers of American whiskey have trouble differentiating brands.

In researching this topic, I divided the dozens of American whiskey brands into two broad categories: Kentucky whiskeys, by which I mean those made by large corporations in and around Kentucky, and craft whiskeys, produced by microdistilleries across the country. Of the Kentucky whiskeys, I gathered the major distilleries on (or formerly on) the Kentucky Bourbon Trail and attempted to plot the brands made at each plant. It was not easy. Most of these distilleries make three types of bourbon mash—one flavored with rye, one flavored with a little more rye, and a third flavored with wheat—and develop different products by aging those three mash bills to meet various grades and price points. For instance, the Jim Beam distillery also makes Booker's, Baker's, Basil

AN AMERICAN WHISKEY FAMILY TREE

This chart shows the major distilleries operating in Kentucky, Tennessee, and Indiana, grouped horizontally by corporate owner, then subdivided by distillery. Each tree shows the type of whiskey made, and the various expressions of each style of whiskey or mash bill, in the case of bourbons. For instance, Basil Hayden's is a longer-aged version of Old Grand-Dad, and both are made at the Jim Beam Distillery. Some of this is imprecise. Buffalo Trace has two bourbon mash bills, but it

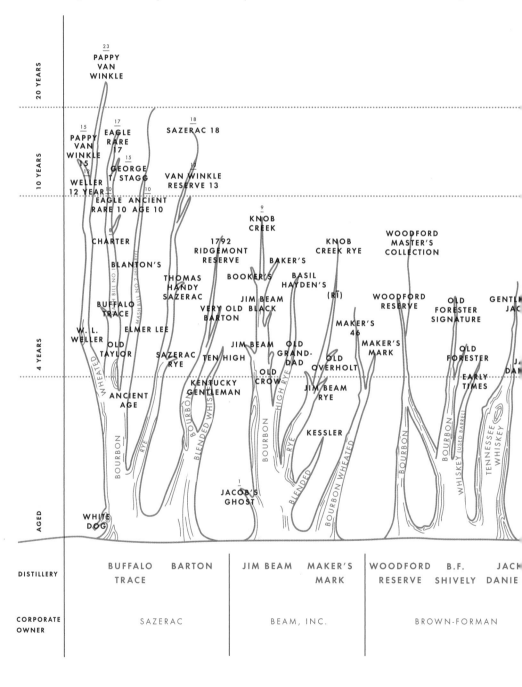

DISTILLERY	BUFFALO TRACE	BARTON	JIM BEAM	MAKER'S MARK	WOODFORD RESERVE	B.F. SHIVELY	JACK DANIE
CORPORATE OWNER	SAZERAC		BEAM, INC.		BROWN-FORMAN		

isn't known which of its many brands are made from each, so this is a rough guess based on online commentary. Willett, formerly only a bottler as Kentucky Bourbon Distillers, has been distilling its own product for about a year; I include the brands that it bottles from other sources for reference. The ages are taken from published age statements if they exist; if they don't, brands have been plotted in the general area where I would guess they belong.

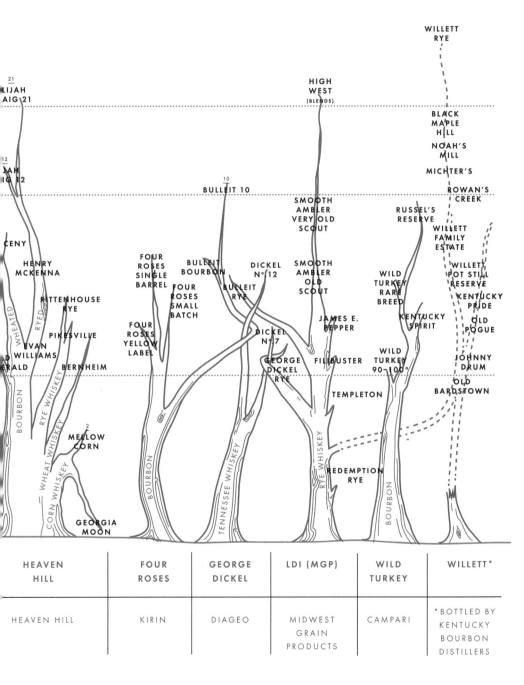

Hayden's, and Knob Creek, as well as Old Crow and Old Grand-Dad. Booker's, Baker's, and Knob Creek probably all use the same Jim Beam formula, and are aged and bottled in slightly different expressions. Basil Hayden's is a premium version of Old Grand-Dad, both of which use the formula with more rye. Old Crow and Jim Beam at one point were the same liquid; they may still be. Jim Beam Black is aged eight years, Baker's seven, and Knob Creek nine. But they are made with the same grain that comes in on the same railcars, mashed in the same ingredient ratios, distilled on the same stills, and aged in the same warehouses.

Across Kentucky, there are far fewer stills than there are whiskey brands. In fact, only six Kentucky bourbons are made at distilleries that bear the same name as the brand: Four Roses, Jim Beam, Woodford Reserve, Maker's Mark, Buffalo Trace, and Wild Turkey. (Heaven Hill is also technically a brand, but it has very limited distribution.) There is Buffalo Trace and there is the version of Buffalo Trace that is called Blanton's and the versions called Eagle Rare, George Stagg, Ancient Age, and even the beloved Pappy Van Winkle, which is really an aged version of W. L. Weller, the Buffalo Trace wheated bourbon base product.

When people ask me, as a distiller, to recommend a Kentucky bourbon, I'm always a little bit at a loss. I like Elijah Craig, which is probably a longer aged Evan Williams, both made by Heaven Hill. Woodford Reserve is made in a handsome distillery, but the pot stills on view produce only a portion of what is put into bottles. I like Bulleit Bourbon, but there is no Bulleit distillery.

Who cares? It's not as if anyone visits the Red Bull factory and insists on inspecting the tanks to make sure it's not producing Monster in the same facility. And I sometimes think it doesn't matter at all, that the whiskey itself should be the measure of the brand. But we also live in a time when we decide what to drink based on more than just taste. Whiskey marketers know this well—hence all the tedious texts on the back of bourbon bottles that reference historical figures and provide vague descriptions of authoritative quality. Rather than offering information about the key determinants of a whiskey's character— the sourcing of ingredients, the mash bills, the still types and aging

Barrels waiting to be loaded into the heated warehouse at Woodford Reserve.

processes—many distilleries simply state how handcrafted each bottle is and how much integrity they have.

Federal laws mandate that certain information appear on whiskey labels, but the results can confuse as much as illuminate. Geographic identifiers can be misleading. (The Pappy Van Winkle bottle says "bottled by Old Rip Van Winkle Distillery, Frankfort, Kentucky," despite the fact that there is no such distillery, that Pappy is now distilled at Buffalo Trace, and that the bourbon in its oldest variant was made in Louisville.) And a whiskey's alcohol percentage (required) and age (conditionally required) can take on outsized significance, as if these were the best indications of quality—sit a barrel for a little longer and dilute it a little less before you bottle it, and you've got a top-shelf product, even though the liquid is the same stuff as your cheapest brand.

Many large distillers have become industrialized to the point that their factories are unrecognizable as distilleries. The traditional copper pot still—in Scotland, mandated as the only equipment for making single malt whiskey—has been replaced in the United States by a maze of pipes, conduits, and rectifying towers that bears more resemblance to an oil refinery. Jim Beam, to its credit, publishes its process flowchart, but I have trouble locating the step in the process where the whiskey is born—I just see chillers and heat exchangers and rectifying trays. This is surely why the big distillers focus their marketing on the post-barrel side of the process, since aging length and proof levels are the easiest variables to adjust.

The rapid rise of craft distilleries and the proliferation of alternative whiskey brands may lead to greater transparency and a more informed public. LDI, for instance, is now planning to host tours of its once highly secretive Lawrenceburg facility. But LDI has also publicized six new mash bills designed specifically to meet the growing demands from "craft distilleries" that want to source whiskey, rather than make their own, which suggests that deliberate obfuscation in the whiskey business may be a tactic younger distilleries are happy to inherit.

I don't mean to be too much of a crank about this. There is more to whiskey than where it is made, and looking for variety might be a more meaningful search than looking for integrity. For our part, we started a distillery because we wanted to make whiskey, not because we thought commercial whiskey was such a disappointment that the public needed an alternative. In fact, duplicitous branding aside, there are plenty of Kentucky whiskeys that are fantastic, and some of the least transparent taste the best.

On the following pages, I've outlined the Kentucky whiskey landscape, focusing on bourbons and other whiskeys that genuinely offer something different or distinctive or terrific. If you're interested in learning more, I recommend Chuck Cowdery's website as the paramount guide to bourbon on the Internet. He has an ornery attitude, which can be rewarding if you agree with him, which I mostly do. He and other online enthusiasts have taken to breaking down some of the marketing myths of the industry, and I have done my best not to repeat the mistakes of others, but my opinions are based on my own perceptions and preferences. In a few instances, I've repeated a story that stretches credibility without being outright false, if the story itself is worth telling.

Heaven Hill's Bardstown distillery was destroyed by fire; all that remains are the aging warehouses along Loretto Road and a bottling plant.

Heaven Hill
BARDSTOWN, KENTUCKY

Heaven Hill is one of my favorite distilleries in Kentucky. Unlike the other distilleries in the state, the company is a privately owned family business that has been passed down for generations since the repeal of Prohibition. The first master distiller was Joseph Beam, the cousin of Jim, who knew he was too far removed to inherit the Beam family legacy and so opened his own distillery instead, in partnership with the Shapira brothers. The Shapiras continue to own and manage the business side of the distillery while Joseph's son and grandson, Parker and Craig Beam, supervise the distilling.

Heaven Hill's Bardstown Distillery was destroyed by fire in 1996, so all of its spirit produced today is made in the Bernheim Distillery in Louisville and trucked to Bardstown, where it is aged and bottled. The distillery's primary brands are **Evan Williams** and **Elijah Craig**, though the company also has a niche in ridiculously marketed brands like **Fighting Cock** and **Georgia Moon** (it is distilled in Louisville), a mason-jar-bottled brand of corn whiskey that is perhaps a deliberately offensive contribution to the category. I said as much in the presence of Max and Andy Shapira once, not realizing who I was talking to, but Max good-naturedly replied with the brand's tagline—"First you swaller, then you holler"—and I suddenly understood pretty much everything I needed to know about their company. In a business where bourbon marketing is mostly conservative and respectful, they seem to be having a good time.

Heaven Hill makes two other brands worth mentioning. **Bernheim** is the only straight wheat whiskey on the market today, and makes an interesting contribution to any whiskey collection. It has a softer, familiar wheat flavor that doesn't need a lot of wood to get a nice balance. I once experimented making wheat whiskeys for about three months, trying to get something as good, but I failed, so I hold it in esteem. There is also **Mellow Corn**, a straight corn whiskey. It has been aged for at least two years (as the term "straight" connotes) in used bourbon barrels. It is much nicer than its cousin, Georgia Moon, and its classic packaging and low price make it a very lovely bottle to keep around. It is also a good example of something between a white whiskey and a straight bourbon, which makes it a useful reference for the home distiller.

Woodford Reserve is made at a historic distillery in Versailles, Kentucky, that has also been known as the Labrot & Graham Distillery and the Old Oscar Pepper Distillery. Distilling at the site dates to the late 1700s.

Brown-Forman
LOUISVILLE, KENTUCKY

Brown-Forman traces its history to Louisville in the 1870s, when the Brown Brothers started blending bourbon whiskey and bottling it in sealed containers. Brown-Forman's best-known bourbon is **Woodford Reserve**, which is partially distilled at the Woodford Reserve Distillery in Versailles (pronounced ver-SAYLES), Kentucky. This is the most beautiful operating distillery in the United States. When I first visited, about ten years ago, the distillery had just opened to the public after a substantial renovation to coincide with the launch of the brand (curiously, they had plenty of aged bourbon, even though the distillery had been open only a few months). The stone stillhouse has three gooseneck pot stills made by Forsyths, the same Scottish manufacturer that made Kings County's stills and most of the ones at distilleries in Scotland. The tour includes a lot of informative history and is more clearly illustrative of the distilling process than other tours on the Kentucky Bourbon Trail. The scale of what you see on the tour is somewhat deceptive, however. Our guide conceded that, to meet demand, the brand pulls barrels from the Brown-Forman Distillery in Louisville. Brown-Forman has also just announced a $35-million expansion of the Woodford Reserve Distillery, so this may change in time.

Master Distiller Chris Morris also makes the **Woodford Reserve Master's Collection**, which is a series of experimental batches that manipulate one variable in the production of classic Woodford Reserve. Master's Collection has finished its bourbon in maple barrels, fermented a sweet mash instead of a sour mash, and aged in used barrels instead of new. Morris is also experimenting with barreling at non-standard proofs, something I'm especially curious about. There are more batches planned, and since they age as long as nine years, there is a fair amount of anticipation that accompanies each release.

Brown-Forman's Louisville distillery is located in the Shively neighborhood and is not open to the public. It dates from the 1940s and has a Cold War munitions factory aesthetic. The primary product produced there is **Early Times**, one of the few Kentucky whiskeys aged in used cooperage, and therefore not technically a bourbon. Early Times is designed to be an inexpensive whiskey. There isn't a longer-aged, higher-priced version, but there should be.

Also produced in Shively is **Old Forester**, which is Brown-Forman's lower-priced legitimate bourbon, though it has the same mash bill as Woodford Reserve and some of its barrels become Woodford Reserve. Old Forester is the oldest brand of bourbon in continuous production, introduced by George Garvin Brown in the 1870s and recognized for being packaged exclusively in sealed bottles only at the distillery, which was an innovation at the time and is now a legal mandate for distillers—you can't sell it to customers by the barrel anymore, unfortunately.

Brown-Forman also owns **Jack Daniel's**, which was started by its namesake distiller in the 1870s and is now the largest-selling American whiskey in the world. Jack Daniel's is a Tennessee whiskey, which is differentiated from bourbon only in that it is made in Tennessee and filtered through maple charcoal before aging, a method known as the Lincoln County Process. This gives it a stronger wood character than bourbon aged for the same amount of time. It's sort of cheating, since it makes the whiskey taste somewhat more mature than it is; but they've been doing it for 140 years, so it's hard to argue that they are doing it wrong.

Jim Beam's Clermont distillery is one of two facilities that produce spirits for all its whiskey brands. Jim Beam White Label is the world's largest bourbon brand.

Beam, Inc.
DEERFIELD, ILLINOIS

Beam, Inc. is an international conglomerate that owns several liquor brands, including Laphroaig, Ardmore, Canadian Club, Sauza tequila, and Courvoisier. The company is best known, though, for its American whiskeys, which include Jim Beam and Maker's Mark.

A visit to the Jim Beam distillery is somewhat like being trapped in an Arby's for an hour and fifteen minutes, while you wait to be served an ounce of cheap whiskey. The recently opened American Stillhouse visitors' center offers two floors of branding, an elevator designed to look like a column still, a video family tree set to bluegrass music, and a lot of corrugated metal.

The tour itself is not so bad. They have an amusing, cartoonish "microdistillery" set up in an entry hall, with miniature stills and five hundred gallons of fermenting mash so as to show visitors how the process works (it is exactly the scale of Kings County, using some of the same Vendome equipment we use). It is fully functional, and our guide told us that the whiskey gets folded into Beam's regular production.

You won't learn much on the tour, but the bottling line is mesmerizing and a remarkable feat of engineering. There are some cringe-inducing, hands-on interactive moments, as when our guide allowed visitors to dump different grains into the baby mash cooker or roll barrels to dump them on "the porch." The highlight is watching thousands of gallons of spirit gushing from the tailboxes beneath the double, six-story rectifying columns—and this is only at the smaller, Clermont facility. Most of Jim Beam is made down the road in Boston, Kentucky.

Jim Beam, the namesake behind the brand, is, according to legend, the fourth distiller in the family line, which stretches back to the 1770s. Beam's grandson Booker Noe was master distiller in recent times and launched the small batch collection. Fred Noe, his son, is the seventh generation of distillers in the family.

Jim Beam White Label is the most widely sold bourbon on the planet, and there's not much to say about it beyond that. There are many partisans lingering in whiskey chat rooms who feel that this bourbon is much maligned and deserves respect for its great value. I am not one of them.

That said, Jim Beam's lines get more interesting at the margins: the highbrow "small batch collection" and the lowbrow classics that have filled the liquor cabinets of ornery, cheap old men for decades. The distillery makes four top-shelf spirits that are fairly ubiquitous: **Booker's**, **Baker's**, **Basil Hayden's**, and **Knob Creek**. Basil Hayden's is a high-rye recipe. Knob Creek is one of the better values if you like a very wood-dominant, high-proof whiskey. Booker's is bottled at barrel strength—the percent alcohol when it emerges from the barrel, which can be anywhere from 121 to 127 proof—and is one of the few commercial whiskeys to pack that much of a kick.

The bottom-shelf brands are even more interesting. Shortly into my career as a distiller, I was given a bottle of **Old Grand-Dad** that was probably produced in the early 1980s. I doubt the product has changed since the production of that bottle, which had a sharp bite but was remarkably sweet. The cap had a bottled-in-bond stamp, and while few whiskeys opt for this certification today, it's a reminder of the fights that legitimate distillers waged against rectifiers in the late 1800s to develop a government-sanctioned set of rules that determined a whiskey's integrity. Mr. Basil Hayden is the particular granddad pictured on the bottle, and both whiskeys share a high-rye mash bill.

To write about **Old Crow** is to write about Dr. James Crow, a Scotsman who studied chemistry and medicine before moving to the United States. He arrived in Kentucky around 1820 and took a scientific approach to distilling at the old Oscar Pepper Distillery (now Woodford Reserve). Dr. Crow used thermometers, hydrometers, and litmus tests to analyze each stage in the distillation process. He was so innovative, he is sometimes miscredited with inventing the sour mash process, which existed in George Washington's day. Dr. Crow kept meticulous logs of his operation, and though his distillery was never very productive, Old Crow had such a good reputation that it endured long after Crow passed away. The brand has been favored by Henry Clay, Ulysses S. Grant, Mark Twain, and Hunter S. Thompson.

Before Jim Beam was made by the family member whose name it now bears, it was called Old Tub. A brand of inexpensive whiskey called **Old Tub** is still sold at the Jim Beam Experience, bottled only in plastic 375-ml bottles to cater to those who want the most from the Experience that money can buy.

More recently, following the explosive interest in white whiskey, Beam came out with something called **Jacob's Ghost**, which is Jim Beam aged for one year and then heavily filtered to remove color and some volatile compounds that are usually aged out by the wood. I was surprised to like this quite a bit. It's not as flavorful as a traditional white whiskey, but it is very easy to drink and a good starter among white whiskeys.

The Beam brands mentioned above are all made at either the company's Clermont or Boston facilities. But just down the road in Loretto is another well-known distillery owned by Beam, Inc.: **Maker's Mark**, whose legend is one of the best in bourbon history. According to lore, the Samuels family, from north of Bardstown, had been in the distilling business going back generations. After Prohibition, T. W. Samuels attempted to get back into the game, but financial pressures related to World War II and a stubborn unwillingness to innovate forced the distillery to close. Then in the 1950s, T. W.'s son, Bill Samuels Sr., together with his wife, Margie, decided to give the family business another shot, determined not to make the same mistakes as his father. Samuels didn't have time to distill all the variations he was considering for his mash bill (I guess he was busy?), so he baked the different options into loaves of bread. The bakery taste test led the family to choose wheat rather than rye as the flavor grain, which led to a softer, mellower whiskey than his rye-dominated competitors. Bill acquired the Burks Spring Distillery and set about making the brand that would become Maker's Mark. His wife, Margie, is given roughly equal billing in the creation myth, as she came up with the brand, drew its logo, and conceived of the red wax dipping. Maker's Mark took time to catch on, but clever advertising in the 1980s helped propel the brand and the bourbon to rapid growth.

Maker's Mark is sometimes described as sweeter than other bourbons, as the wheat allows more of the corn and malt to interact with barrel sugars. Maker's recently came out with **Maker's 46**, a variant that ages regular Maker's Mark a few extra months with French oak staves inserted in the barrel. This version, not surprisingly, is a little more woody, but not radically different.

Last year, facing record demand and limited supply, Maker's Mark announced that they would reduce the proof of their whiskey to 42 percent alcohol by volume, down from 45 percent. This caused fans of the product to revolt. Although Jack Daniel's and other equally beloved spirits had done the same thing a few years earlier, Maker's Mark drew especially harsh criticism and backtracked a week later, saying they would keep the product at 45 percent and manage the inevitable product shortage.

The gardens in front of the Elmer T. Lee Clubhouse at Buffalo Trace, on the banks of the Kentucky River. The brick tower just left of center holds the 60,000-gallon-capacity stills.

Buffalo Trace

FRANKFORT, KENTUCKY

Buffalo Trace is a distillery owned by Sazerac, a privately held company based in Metairie, Louisiana, that traces its history back to the 1870s, when New Orleans was still a port where whiskey barrels were actively traded. The company began as a bar in the French Quarter known as the Sazerac Coffee House, which invented the Sazerac cocktail, often described as the first mixed drink. Today, it operates distilleries in Frankfort and Bardstown, and the A. Smith Bowman Distillery in Virginia.

Buffalo Trace is the flagship brand produced by a historic distillery in Frankfort that has been operating under various names along the banks of the Kentucky River, just north of the state capital, for nearly two and a half centuries. The distillery was one of a handful allowed to stay open during Prohibition for the production of "medicinal" whiskey. A prescription allowed for a half-pint every ten days, and the thirteen years of Prohibition coincided with an alarming uptick in ailments— whole families falling victim to various, highly contagious conditions that required multiple prescriptions for each household. The Buffalo Trace brand has only been around since 1999, but other historic brands, such as Ancient Age, have been made on the site for much longer.

Buffalo Trace is the largest Kentucky distillery not listed on the Kentucky Bourbon Trail, and reservations are required to see the interior of the factory. But the distillery is worth visiting, and the hard-hat tour they offer is the most in-depth of the distillery tours I experienced. Master Distiller Harlen Wheatley has set up a small trial still where he produces the experimental collection: a series of limited-run bourbons that play with unorthodox grains and alternative aging techniques. The bottles are highly coveted, and one wonders why Buffalo Trace doesn't devote more still capacity to these experiments instead of pumping out more of the same minor variations on a well-worn theme from the big still.

Buffalo Trace seems to have a particularly nasty attitude toward craft distillers, issuing press releases that tout the results of easily debunked experiments that "prove" the intrinsic value of the status quo regarding barrel size and aging techniques that happen to coincide with exactly their process. And yet the company has what appears to be a genuine interest in distilled-spirits research. Buffalo Trace recently built a new warehouse where they can control many variables that affect the aging process, potentially isolating the effects of heat, humidity, light, and air currents, and one hopes this further develops the available science of aging.

Blanton's is probably Buffalo Trace's most well-known top-shelf bourbon. It is described in marketing materials as the first "single barrel" whiskey. This was something of a novelty in 1984, when the brand was first introduced. Originally, the idea was that in the course of making the distillery's workhorse spirits, the master blender may come across a remarkable barrel worth special attention. This would be set aside and bottled independently (as legend goes, for Colonel Blanton's personal use when he was president of the Frankfort Distillery). These days, with many top-shelf bourbons competing for attention with essentially the same narrative—special barrels, hand picked—the concept of the single barrel means very little, and it can be easy to forget that Blanton's was an early pioneer.

Buffalo Trace sells its new make, or unaged, spirit in half-size bottles from three variants of Buffalo Trace mash bills at what would be barrel-entry strength, which are simply branded as **Buffalo Trace White Dog**. To me, this product is the best example of how large distilleries and small distilleries differ in terms of the spirit they produce. Dilute it down to a more palatable proof and it still has intense notes that are hard to get around. It's a helpful illustration of how spirit that goes into the barrel with a lot of imperfection can come out quite nicely— you barely recognize the rough notes of the white dog in their finished bourbon—and they should be given credit for even releasing their base white spirit, something only a few other distilleries have done.

    Pappy Van Winkle is frequently described by both educated and uneducated drinkers as the best bourbon on the market. It is certainly aged for longer than most premium bourbons, and has earned a near hysterical following of people scrambling to get one of the very few bottles that are released each year. I remember drinking Pappy years ago when it was merely an especially good bourbon with clever, idiosyncratic branding. Now, people I barely know send me Facebook messages asking where they can find Pappy, as if I, a distiller in New York City, am somehow holding a supply that I might offload at a markup. Suffice it to say, Pappy has always been very good whiskey; of the long-aged bourbons, it seems to be aged very gently year-to-year, and this recommends it enormously. But in blind taste tests by people I trust, it does not beat out younger, less expensive bourbons. I'd love to run that test for myself, but, like everyone else, I can't find a bottle anywhere.

    Buffalo Trace also makes a wide variety of other brands, which, at the high end (**Eagle Rare, George T. Stagg, E. H. Taylor, Thomas H. Handy Rye**) become superlative for the sake of being superlative; the company has many top-shelf bourbons and it can be hard to differentiate them. One noteworthy line is **W. L. Weller**, a well-aged wheated bourbon that is offered in a variety of bottlings, and whose twelve-year is excellent and reasonably priced.

The Four Roses Distillery dates to 1910 and is on the National Register of Historic Places.

Four Roses

LAWRENCEBURG, KENTUCKY

Four Roses is a beautiful little distillery in a wooded valley located adjacent to the Salt River. Built in a Spanish style in 1910, the distillery changed hands several times and was finally bought by Kirin, the Japanese beverage company. Before Kirin took over, it was impossible to get Four Roses straight bourbon in the United States; the brand's previous owner sold it only for export to Japan. Now the brand is having a renaissance. Four Roses has an interesting, probably overly complex, strategy of taking two mash bills and five yeast strains and playing out those permutations into small batch and single barrel offerings based on the different flavors that emerge. The story behind the bourbon is that Paul Jones Jr., founder of the brand in 1888, offered a proposal of marriage to his sweetheart, asking her to wear roses to a ball to signify her acceptance. She wore a corsage of four red roses, and her commitment inspired the whiskey, though one account calls foul because Jones died a bachelor.

George Dickel is made in Cascade Hollow, near Tullahoma, Tennessee.

Diageo
LONDON, ENGLAND

Bulleit is the primary bourbon made by Diageo, the beverage giant that owns Johnnie Walker, Smirnoff, and Guinness, and all of its bourbon is surely made by contract at Four Roses, though this is technically speculative since brand representatives refuse to confirm. However, they tout Salt River water and single-story warehousing, both specific to Four Roses. Like many of Diageo's brands, Bulleit is mostly a branding story, but the bourbon is good for the price. Coincidentally, Bulleit Rye is made at LDI in Lawrenceburg, Indiana, and Bulleit Bourbon at Four Roses in Lawrenceburg, Kentucky, but the two towns are unrelated geographically.

Diageo also owns **George Dickel**, the main alternative Tennessee whiskey to Jack Daniel's. Its **Number 12** is a personal favorite. For years, if you wanted Tennessee whiskey, you had only two brands to pick from, so they had a run on the category. There are more Tennessee whiskeys cropping up, but Dickel will remain a sentimental and traditional preference. Dickel now also makes a rye, and like Bulleit Rye, it's produced at the LDI distillery in Indiana.

CRAFT WHISKEYS

In the 1980s, entrepreneur John Torgersen worked as a sea captain on marine vessels and oil rigs in the North Sea, off the coast of Scotland. During his free time, he visited distilleries there, noting how the whiskey makers in small towns grew micro-economies of farms and supportive businesses around them. Years later, he found himself living in Schoharie County, New York, on the far side of the Catskill Mountains from the Hudson Valley, surrounded by cornfields and a depressed economy. He thought to make corn whiskey from heirloom, open-pollinated corn that he researched with experts from Cornell University's agricultural program. But there was a sticking point. New York State wanted $39,575 for a three-year license, which was more than Torgersen could afford without major investment. He just wanted to make white corn whiskey, in the old way, on a farm distillery. His operation would be called Storm King Distillery, after the mighty mountain that serves as a gateway to the Hudson Highlands.

There were already a few other small distilleries. The state had an existing provision for a brandy distiller's license, which was much less expensive—around $250—and in New York, as in California, Washington, and other wine-producing states, some vintners were throwing wine into an alembic still to make eau-de-vie and brandy. Stills had been operating at Knapp Vineyards and Swedish Hill Winery since 1994 and 1996, respectively, but their output was very small and served to support the larger winery business. A stand-alone distillery hadn't yet been considered in New York, and certainly not one making whiskey.

Torgersen got in touch with his local farm bureau office to see what could be done about the fees. Bureau chief John Radcliffe became interested and passed his idea to the state's main office, which eventually championed legislative action. Despite opposition from the distributors' lobby, a bill allowing for a new class of license, the A-1, with a production cap and a reduced fee, gradually worked through the Senate and the Assembly and was signed by Governor George Pataki in 2002.

By this time, Torgersen had moved on. He had never been able to get his business together—bad luck, bad timing, and a divorce conspired against him—and he now lives in Houston, working in quality and safety assurance for maritime oil and gas drilling. But all the distilleries that currently populate New York State owe Torgersen, the aspiring entrepreneur, for our existence. In 2005, Ralph Erenzo and Brian Lee started making the heirloom corn whiskey that Torgersen had dreamed of by securing the state's first A-1 license. Since then, dozens of distilleries have opened, making vodka, brandy, gin, rum, applejack, whiskey, eau-de-vie, liqueurs, and even absinthe, and many of them are distilling spirits from New York–grown agricultural products.

New York was not the first state to license microdistilleries, but it was an important one, and other states have since followed. More than two hundred new distilleries have been established across the United States since 2000. Every month, it seems, another new distillery opens its doors, trumpeting the return of whiskey and other spirits to another corner of the country. All but five states have seen a small distillery open in what is becoming the craft model—and surely there are more coming, along with a cavalcade of new brands. Already there are more craft whiskeys available to the discerning customer than the Kentucky whiskeys discussed above.

The word *craft* is not one I particularly like, since the mainstream bourbon industry has already co-opted it and rendered it almost meaningless. But this is true of other microdistillery terms, too. Massive distillers occasionally still use *small batch* to refer to the culling of a limited number of barrels from the warehouse, even though in many cases, these so-called small batches are larger than most craft distillers' yearly output. Small producers are often scrambling for meaningful words to describe what they do.

The new copper pot stills at Kings County, shortly after their arrival from Scotland.

There is a genuine difference, though, between the Kentucky and craft whiskeys, which has to do, more than anything else, with their respective freedoms and constraints. Kentucky whiskeys are mostly made by large, mature, cautious companies wary of altering their business. Craft whiskeys are made by young, small, underfinanced companies with every incentive to experiment. And so the best way to appreciate the emerging craft-whiskey landscape is to look for the distillers with obvious creativity—the ones who smoke their own malt, who distill from grains you barely recognize as grains, and who obtain special label approvals for products that don't fit into easy categories; the distillers that focus necessarily on ingredients and tight distillation cuts rather than age and proof. What follows is my attempt to sort through the most interesting examples of whiskey being made by small distillers, categorized by defining characteristic. This is by no means a comprehensive list, and is bound to miss some great products, but it is meant as a start.

THE PIONEERS

St. George, founded in 1982 by Alsace native Jörg Rupf, probably has the best claim to being the first craft distillery in the United States. Located in a former airplane hangar in Alameda, California, the distillery has an iconic quality, with gleaming German hybrid stills arranged in an L shape on platforms over a cavernous, skylit space. In 2000, the distillery launched Hangar One Vodka, its most well known product, though it had already been making eau-de-vie and **St. George Single Malt Whiskey**. After ten years, it sold off the Hangar One brand (though they still produce it under contract), and the distillery now focuses again on their original interests of fruit brandies and whiskey. (Its bourbon brand, **Breaking & Entering**, is sourced from Kentucky.)

This focus on fruit-based distillation was common among the early West Coast spirits producers. **Germain-Robin** started around the same time as St. George, in Ukiah, California, though it did not start producing until 1983. Its founders, Ansley Coale, a local rancher, and Hubert Germain-Robin, a distiller from the Cognac region of France, launched the company with a grape brandy something more like cognac, with different varietals than the traditional ugni-blanc grape. In 1986, in Portland, Oregon, **Clear Creek** started producing its own pear eau-de-vie on German hybrid stills. Both of these distilleries also make whiskey on their stills. Germain-Robin has recently started to produce **Low Gap Whiskey** from malted wheat on its traditional alembic cognac-style still, and Clear Creek has long been known for a peated single malt scotch-style whiskey that is highly coveted, and is probably the best known of the West Coast brandy distilleries' whiskey offerings.

Then there is **Anchor Distilling Company**, founded in 1993 by the company that makes Anchor Steam beer, and located in the same facility in San Francisco. Anchor's **Old Potrero Whiskey** is a rye aged in uncharred oak, which remains very unusual among craft distillers. They also make a straight rye whiskey and a long-aged version under the Old Potrero brand. Their Junipero gin is somewhat better known, and their Genevieve gin is more of a Dutch-style genever—essentially a gin made from white whiskey instead of vodka.

St. George's reconfigured airplane hangar in Alameda, California.

In 1989, George Stranahan was a microbrewer living in Woody Creek, Colorado, not far from Kentuckian and whiskey enthusiast Hunter S. Thompson. During a barn fire on his property, Stranahan met volunteer firefighter Jess Graber, who made corn whiskey as a hobby. One day, Graber loaded some of Stranahan's microbrew into his still. The experiment was so successful that Stranahan offered to set up the still in one of the outbuildings on his ranch (presumably a metal one) and the **Stranahan's** brand was born. The distillery eventually moved to Denver and began taking its wash from Flying Dog Brewery. Stranahan's is unusual in that it's a straight barley-based whiskey, and still has a relatively limited production, even though the brand was one of the first craft distilleries to be sold.

I categorize **Death's Door** as a pioneer not because it was particularly early on the scene, or an interesting company—it was contract-distilling all of its products until last year, when it opened a new facility in Middleton, Wisconsin. I give credit to Death's Door as the first distillery to make an inexpensive white whiskey as a cocktail mixer. It helped launch the category and was soon to be popular in New York bars and restaurants. Made from wheat, Death's Door's white whiskey is a little more like vodka than you'd want from a white whiskey, but cocktail makers have found it less mystifying than more robust white spirits.

And finally, there is one of New York's first distilleries, **Warwick Valley**. In 2002, Jeremy Kidde moved east from San Francisco to join the business team of a small winery west of the Hudson River, just north of New York City. He was aware of Clear Creek and some of the other wineries making fruit brandies on the West Coast, and thought something similar could be possible in New York State's wine-growing regions, too. Kidde applied for the state's Class C license, which allowed him to make only fruit brandies, and set to work developing a range of products. Then he conducted a customer tasting session at Astor Wines, New York City's most prominent liquor store. He sold maybe ten or twelve bottles. At the end of the tasting, he asked the sales staff how many cases of Trimbach (the most respected brand of *poire william*, a pear brandy from France) they sold each year. "About two cases," they said—only two times what he'd just sold in an afternoon. Kidde returned to Warwick and filed for a license to make something more popular. The distillery began contract-distilling for other startup distilleries looking to source spirits, as well as making their own **Black Dirt** bourbon; its greatly expanded whiskey facility is now completely independent of the winery and will begin production soon.

THE INNOVATORS

Many microdistilleries tweak ingredients or production techniques, but these four have established a reputation for unusual curiosity. **Balcones**, in Waco, Texas, is best known for its blue corn whiskeys; an extremely well-regarded single malt whiskey; and something called rumble, which is a sort of rum made with honey and figs in the mash that falls outside the normal classes of spirit (it is called a "distilled spirits specialty" by the Alcohol and Tobacco Tax and Trade Bureau [TTB]). Founder and head distiller Chip Tate built much of the distillery's equipment himself. He has experience in brewing but this fortunately stays in the background with the whiskeys. While some former brewers can't seem to escape their roots—the proliferation of pointlessly hopped whiskeys being one example—Chip makes imaginative whiskey that springs from the scrubby Texas landscape.

Darek Bell, his wife, Amy, and their partner, Andrew Webber, started **Corsair Artisan Distillery**, which operates out of two locations: Nashville, Tennessee, and Bowling Green, Kentucky. Corsair's whiskeys are adventurous. They include a quinoa whiskey, a triple smoked malt whiskey (cherrywood, peat, and beechwood), a couple of rye whiskeys, some moonshine infusions, red absinthe—and these are just the regular, non-seasonal releases. Corsair's primary still is one of the most interesting in craft distilling: a salvaged copper gin still that looks like something from a Dr. Seuss book. While the branding is a little aggressive (like a movie poster for *Reservoir Dogs*), the spirits are given high marks from tough critics. Bell also wrote a book on spirits recipes for small distillers that is as generous and transparent as the big distilleries are polished and guarded.

The **New Holland Brewery and Distillery**, in Holland, Michigan, is located not far from the DeKlomp Wooden Shoe and Delft Factory (which advertises tulips, wooden shoes, delft tiles, and bison meat) and Dutch Village, a particularly terrifying amusement park from my youth with a giant wooden shoe you could climb inside and slide down that smelled improbably like feet. It makes beer and whiskey in a large nondescript warehouse facility, and then serves from its down-

The repurposed gin still at Corsair Artisan Distillery in Nashville.

town brewpub. The distillery has a six-hundred-gallon still salvaged from a defunct New Jersey distillery that runs in a separate building. They have a sourced bourbon that they then age in beer barrels that once held the brewery's Dragon's Milk Stout, which itself is aged in used bourbon barrels from Kentucky. While the bourbon in this product is sourced from Kentucky for now, their distillery-made malt whiskies, led by **Zeppelin Bend** and **Brewer's Whiskey**, are much better and show the skills of the distiller. They also have something that they were trying to call hopquila, a hops- and sugar-infused white whiskey, though as my guide mentioned, "There were complaints from the cartel."

Koval was founded in 2008 by Robert and Sonat Birnecker, a husband and wife who left academic careers to start a distillery in Chicago focused on organic spirits. Robert's grandparents had a history of winemaking and distilling back in Austria, and he wanted to rekindle the family tradition. While some distillers pay lip service to using organic ingredients in their whiskeys, Koval's **Lion's Pride** whiskeys are all certified organic and kosher. Each of the five whiskeys is made with a single grain—spelt, millet, wheat, oat, and rye—and sold in three versions: unaged, aged in toasted barrels, and aged in charred barrels. Koval also makes a series of liqueurs, brandies, and eaux-de-vie.

THE HOME TEAM

For decades, Kentucky has been somewhat inhospitable to microdistilleries, but this is changing quickly. **MB Roland**, from St. Elmo, is one of my favorite Kentucky distilleries—it's just a farm with a still on it, not anything fancy or expensive, though they make a wide variety of products, including several unaged whiskeys and a corn and sugar wash moonshine. The distillery was started by Paul Tomaszewski, who was stationed at Fort Campbell, and his wife, Mary Beth, who lived nearby. They decided to start a distillery to make good use of a local farm. The distillery throws "pickin' on the porch" events and camp distillery classes.

Willett Distillery, in Bardstown, is also known as Kentucky Bourbon Distillers. It is technically on the craft distillery trail in Kentucky, though it must certainly be the craft distillery with the largest productive capacity in the country. The Willett family made bourbon since the 1850s and officially as a company since 1935, until the 1970s oil crisis, when the distillery converted to fuel-ethanol production. When crude-oil prices stabilized, the family got out of distilling, and the plant served only as a bottling facility for whiskeys sourced from other distilleries. Last year, the younger generation of the family built a new distillery with a twenty-eight-inch rectification column and a new pot still doubler from Vendome. Willet filled one of their old rickhouses with its first year of production, and gradually will grow stock of its own distilled product. The white dog off the new setup is excellent, bright and buttery, and one can expect in three years to have an excellent Kentucky bourbon. When I visited recently, Janelle Kulsveen (the Willett line took a matriarchal detour and Willetts are now Kulsveens) was working the tasting room, with a future heir to the Willett legacy in a car seat next to the cash register. Labels bottled by Kentucky Bourbon Distillers include: **Johnny Drum, Old Bardstown, Noah's Mill, Rowan's Creek, Pure Kentucky**. A few other brands are bottled for other companies, including **Black Maple Hill, Michter's**, and **Old Pogue**. The distillery's Willett line is for now contracted from elsewhere, though that will likely change when their aging stock comes due.

The historic Pogue House sits on a bluff overlooking the Ohio River in Maysville; the new distillery building can be seen in the foreground.

Alltech, in Lexington, is one of Kentucky's newest distilleries. Started by Pearse Lyons, an Irish-born scientist, Alltech makes nutritional supplements for farm animals, pets, and racehorses. The Alltech website is frankly one of the scariest I've come across on the Internet. In the "Pig Advantage Program," you will find the following text: "Our vision for the pathway to profit includes fine-tuning the pigs' genetic performance and increasing focus on providing solutions that meet the need of the customer and the end consumer." There are bullet points about improved taste, texture, and tenderness; meat that is "naturally fresh"; and providing an end product that is "safe and traceable." Not to pick on Pearse Lyons, though he did name his malt whiskey after himself. His first non-livestock business was a brewery that makes one of the most delicious beers I've ever tasted, Kentucky Bourbon Barrel Ale, a product so coveted that one bar in New York keeps a secret keg he drove up from Kentucky on tap. The distillery, now called **Town Branch**, uses Forsyth copper pot stills, which would recommend it, but the whiskey itself is a little even-tempered for my taste.

Old Pogue is the first distillery to begin operating in the larger, historical Bourbon County in a good long while, and in the town of

Short Mountain has set up an outdoor moonshine still on their property, but most of the distilling is done by a Vendome hybrid still.

Maysville, once known as Limestone, from which much of Bourbon County's whiskey shipped in the early 1800s. There is a familiar story here: a storied distillery that closed with Prohibition, only to be revived several generations later by descendants eager to reclaim the family legacy. The newer version of the distillery is a modern microdistillery, with a limited production; what Pogue sells as its main line is sourced from elsewhere and bottled at Willett.

In 2010, four brothers of the Kaufman family, descendants of the Samsonite luggage concern, decided to plant organic, open-pollinated corn and make estate-grown moonshine in the Tennessee Valley. Right now, **Short Mountain**, in Woodbury, offers corn and sugar mash moonshine and an apple pie variant, though bourbon is on the way. When they had mules plow their cornfield, they made sure to take a lot of pictures, and this kind of attitude has given the brand a highbrow, personality-driven, grassroots character. Metal coins inscribed with the golden rule ("Do unto others as you would have them do unto you") are affixed to every bottle, in a nod to the brothers' great-grandfather, who gave marbles engraved with the same saying to employees of Samsonite.

High West Distillery is more a restaurant than a distillery, though the company has made a name for itself by blending sourced whiskeys.

THE SOURCERS

No distillery that sources its whiskey from elsewhere deserves as much credit as one that makes whiskey itself, but there are some that do their sourcing with unusual care. **High West**, for instance, is a Park City, Utah, distillery with a much larger presence in the market than its distillery would suggest, given that it is really just a restaurant with a small still behind glass upstairs. (The mechanics are tucked away in the basement, and aging, barreling, and bottling take place in nearby Salt Lake City.) High West makes a couple of products that are distilled on site—a white oat whiskey and a rye whiskey—but they also sell a variety of sourced products, many of which come from LDI. Their **Rendezvous Rye**, **Bourye** (a blend of bourbon and rye), and **Campfire** (a blend of bourbon, rye, and scotch) are popular offerings. As a blender and bottler, High West has made a name for itself in sourcing good whiskeys with creative blends that are innovative for their own sake. High West is probably the best example of how a distillery can make the most with limited still capacity, applying the imagination of a craft distiller to the sourcing and blending of other whiskeys.

Other contract distillers seemed to be focused more on branding. If you talk about rye whiskey long enough, someone will bring up **Templeton**. It's a youngish rye, at least when I tried it, bottled out of Iowa and trading on the town of Templeton's reputation during Prohibition for bootleg rye whiskey. Templeton is one of the more deceptive sourcers, marketing a secret "Prohibition-era" recipe as part of its story (it's 95 percent rye, 5 percent malted barley, just like all aged LDI rye), making overtures to being small batch, and name-dropping Al Capone on the bottle. **Smooth Ambler**, from Maxwelton, West Virginia, was founded in 2009 and already has a number of products on the market, including a six- and seven-year-old bourbon and a rye from LDI. These sourced whiskeys are called the **Old Scout** line. The distillers found a few older barrels, which they released as **Very Old Scout**. While acknowledging that these are all "curated" bourbons, Smooth Ambler brands its sourced product very similarly to what is made in-house, and makes no mention of its sourcing on its website.

WhistlePig is another distillery surrounded by talent but—at the moment, at least—selling a sourced whiskey. WhistlePig's rye whiskey is distilled in Canada, even though the brand is based at an organic farm in rural Vermont. Entrepreneur Raj Bhakta, a former *Apprentice* contestant and a one-time Pennsylvanian congressional candidate, launched the brand in 2010, hiring former Maker's Mark master distiller Dave Pickerell, one of the most creative and intelligent minds in the whiskey world. The whiskey is very good and probably worth its price, and belongs in any discussion of excellent sourced whiskeys. But there is no operational WhistlePig distillery in Vermont, and until the company starts making something, WhistlePig is basically just a branding company based at an organic farm.

The stills at Tuthilltown Spirits were reconfigured after a 2012 fire damaged the distillery building.

THE TRADITIONALISTS

Some of the newest distilleries in America are focusing on the oldest, traditional methods. In Mount Vernon, Virginia, George Washington's former distillery has recently been restored, in part through funding by the trade organization that lobbies on behalf of large spirits companies. Today, whiskey is distilled in five reconstructed direct-fire copper pot stills and sold as **Washington's Rye Whiskey** (60 percent rye, 35 percent corn, 5 percent malt). The whiskey, like the whiskey in Washington's day, is sold unaged. The distillery only runs for short periods of time each year, so call ahead if you want to visit while it's in action.

Tuthilltown Spirits, located in New York's Hudson Valley, is one of the largest and most established craft whiskey distilleries. In the early 2000s, founder Ralph Erenzo had plans to build a climbers' ranch at the historic grist mill, located not far from Shawangunk Mountains, which offer some of the best rock climbing in the region. But community members protested, and so Erenzo then turned his attention to whiskey, which seemed to bother the community less. Its

Hudson line of whiskeys includes an all-corn bourbon, a four-grain bourbon, a malt whiskey, and a rye whiskey, as well as a classic corn whiskey. Hudson's squat bottles are widely distributed and, by at least one measure, commercially successful. In 2010, Tuthilltown sold the Hudson brand to the UK-based company William Grant & Sons.

FEW Spirits, in Evanston, Illinois, is named after suffragette and temperance advocate Frances Elizabeth (Catherine) Willard, and has built its labels around the World's Columbian Exposition, the influential World's Fair of 1893 that left a deep impression on architecture and the industrious American interior. **Troy & Sons**, in Asheville, North Carolina, makes its corn whiskey from Crooked Creek Corn, an open-pollinated heirloom white corn that had almost disappeared but is still grown by a small farm a few miles away from the distillery. **Dad's Hat**, in Bristol, Pennsylvania, is devoted to distilling rye whiskey in the state that made the spirit famous in the 1800s. Currently it offers only a white spirit and an aged counterpart, but that might just be enough. Founder Herman Mihalich's family used to run a neighborhood bar, and for him, making a rye whiskey is an homage to that institution.

In the Sunset Park neighborhood of Brooklyn, Brad Estabrooke, a former finance guy who left Wall Street after the 2008 crash, founded **Brueckelen Distilling**. He started by making gin, and then found that the wheat spirit he was producing as the gin's base would make a fine whiskey, too. Estabrooke's **77** whiskeys are exceptional and a good value among craft spirits. He is a meticulous, intelligent distiller, and it shows in his spirits.

The outdoor still at Lost Spirits.

THE OUTLIERS

And then there are the handful of American distilleries that defy categorization: small and quirky enough to appear more like a well-developed hobby than an act of commerce. **House Spirits Distillery**, in Portland, Oregon, is a tiny distillery making squat bottles of white whiskey that are consistently listed among the best in the category. It also offers aged whiskeys as well as other spirits, and even custom barrels, made to customer specifications, starting at around $5,000.

Of all the distilleries in the United States, **Delaware Phoenix** strikes me as the most idiosyncratic. For the first few years of her operation, founder Cheryl Lins macerated her herbs, distilled and hand-bottled her absinthe, and delivered by hand to the best liquor stores and cocktail bars in New York. For her first website, she painted watercolors. Since absinthe went "legal" in 2007, it has mostly attracted distillers who are aiming low. Lins's first absinthes—**Walton Waters** and **Meadow of Love**—are, by contrast, discussed only in whispered reverence among the bartenders I know. The distillery has recently upgraded its still (now to forty-five gallons at a time) and started making whiskey, which is only a little less successful.

The most important thing to know about **Lost Spirits**, in Monterey, California, is that founder Bryan Davis built his own still. That would be something of an achievement on its own and surprisingly rare among craft distillers. However, this particular still resides permanently outdoors, is made of wood, and has a dragon's head that belches steam. Davis has also chosen the most challenging of spirits to make first; he prepares the grains for his peated whiskeys in his own malt smoker. It's carefully made whiskey, certainly unlike anything else around, and is vigorously defended by Davis himself in the comments sections of online review sites. The tasting notes from the whiskey's enthusiasts sound like a trip through a burning jungle cooled with sea spray.

PART 3

SCOTCH

To some extent, the whiskey landscape of Scotland has always been a collection of craft distillers, at least compared to American bourbon distillers. Scotch whisky is more constrained than American whiskey, at least in terms of identification and taxonomy, and especially when it comes to single malts. There is only one ingredient permitted, one type of distillation, and a specific type of aging. But remarkably, despite these constraints, single malts show a lot more variation brand to brand than American whiskey, probably because the constraints have demanded creativity from producers.

One could write an entire volume on Scotch whisky, and it's well beyond the scope of this book, but I think there is an interesting corollary and contrast to American whiskey production. This is especially useful for the home distiller but it is relevant to any drinker of whiskeys because it illustrates some of the debates about process.

The laws governing scotch were rewritten in 2009 to create five types of Scotch whisky, but the two most common, single malt and blended whisky, account for nearly all of the bottles sold in the United States. (The other three are single grain, blended or vatted malt, and blended grain.) **Johnnie Walker, Dewar's,** and **Chivas** are familiar blended whiskey brands, and **Glenmorangie, Macallan, Glenlivet, Ardbeg,** and **Laphroaig** are some of the most well known among single malts. The single malts are pot-distilled whiskies with a lot of flavor; the blended whiskies take single malt whiskies and blend them with what Scotland calls "grain whisky" but what we might call aged vodka: high-proof, column-distilled spirit made from any grain.

In the 1820s, John Walker was a grocer selling whisky in Kilmarnock, Scotland. According to legend, he was frustrated with

The Strathisla distillery, near the River Spey, is the oldest continually operating
distillery in Scotland, founded in 1798 and now owned by Chivas.

the uneven whiskies coming out of the local distilleries and started his
own line. Blended whisky did not become legal in Scotland until 1860;
Walker's son Alexander introduced Walker's Old Highland in 1865.
Alexander had apprenticed as a tea blender in Glasgow, and applied
that experience to the blending of whiskies. The wholesale business in
inexpensive blended whiskies, and the reach of Britain's international
trade, helped catapult Johnnie Walker into the position that it holds
today, as the largest whiskey brand on the planet—it sold eighteen
million cases last year, which is almost double the sales of its nearest
competitor, Jack Daniel's.

Blended whisky spread to the British colonies and beyond,
giving much of the globe a taste for Scottish whisky that was lighter and
more accessible than its heavy, single malt progenitors. This benefitted
the single malt distillers as well as the blenders. Because the blended
whiskies depended on the single malts for flavor, they kept the smaller
distilleries active, and because they required consistency in the taste
profile, a traditional distilling format—malted barley washes, pot still

distillation, and aging in used barrels—was encouraged and eventually codified into law. Still, single malts remained a niche, almost invisible product until the 1970s, when blended-scotch drinkers got interested in the component whiskies, and as wine- and whiskey-tasting events helped stoke a customer base of high-net-worth aficionados.

The "single" in single malt refers to a single distillery; all single malts must be made on the same stills in a single season, which ensures that all whisky in the bottle from a particular brand comes from the same place. In most cases, the names of the distillery and the brand are synonymous, a marked contrast from the American system of one distillery producing several brands. The malt in single malt refers to malted barley, which is the only type of grain that can be used. Traditionally, the barley malt was dried with peat fires, which infused the grains with that peaty flavor (the smokiness of scotch comes from the peat, not the barrel). Today, peat fire is no longer necessary for malting, but most scotches include a little bit of a peaty character to acknowledge this tradition. Scotches from Islay (pronounced EYE-la) have a reputation for being the most peaty (Ardbeg and Laphroaig are common examples of heavily peated scotches).

Single malts must be batch distilled on pot stills. This is yet another distinction from American whiskey, which can be made in continuous stills so long as the proof coming off the still is 160 or less. In America, many distilleries can make whiskey and vodka from the same equipment, simply by adjusting a few of the valves, and very frequently they do. In Scotland, whisky distilleries are simply whisky distilleries. Their pot stills are designed for the low-proof, batch distillation of whisky and wouldn't be useful at making much else.

Finally, scotch must be aged in used barrels (known as "casks" in Scotland), which makes the maturation process two to three times longer than that of American whiskeys. This is mostly due to the fact that, like a tea bag, a barrel infuses more slowly upon each successive use. But there is also Scotland's cooler, more even climate that demands patience. By law, scotch must age for three years, but most rest for much longer and experience extended maturation curves. A twelve-year-old scotch whisky tastes very different from an eighteen, which in turn tastes very different from a twenty-five-year-old. Sherry casks and bourbon barrels are the most common sources for scotch barrels, and they impart slightly different effects over time.

While some Scottish distilleries are quite large—Macallan, Glenlivet, and Glenfiddich each have huge distilleries with rows of stills—many single malts come from small distilleries that have been operating for generations. Because the Scots were very keen to protect their whisky, the laws have sheltered distillers from the type of runaway branding and sourcing that has eroded some of the credibility of American whiskey. While I'm more inclined to drink American whiskey, I appreciate the integrity and variety of scotch, and sometimes I wish that we had similar laws requiring transparency in our bourbon and rye production and labeling.

American whiskeys are so similar from brand to brand that consumers don't notice when a new brand tastes like an existing one, and there is no legal requirement to list the distillery on the bottle (though some geographic provenance is required). One quick improvement would be to require that the geographic provenance be confined to where the product was distilled, or include the DSP (Distilled Spirits Plant) registry number on the bottle. Another solution would be for American distillers, through a trade organization, to agree on something like the *appellation d'origine contrôlée* (AOC), which protects certain classes of French products, as a way to certify a spirit as distilled, bottled, and branded by one producer. On the other hand, this ignores the storytelling aspect of the bourbon tradition, and the fact that brands have always been somewhat invented. To deny the audience the fun of a yarn might be to strip bourbon of the medicine-show hucksterism that is classically American and an undeniable aspect of its history.

This all may soon become a moot point. There are signs that American whiskey is running out. The rate of growth of American bourbon sales jumped 48 percent in 2012, and Maker's Mark's attempt to dilute its spirit may have hardened customers against similar strategies. Buffalo Trace issued a press release saying that they wouldn't dilute their whiskeys or raise their prices "excessively" to cope with the shortage. Heaven Hill is completing an expansion that will add more warehouses to its already impressive complex in Bardstown, though the capacity added remains small relative to the surge in sales last year. Whiskey takes time to age, and if supply runs short, contract bottlers will most likely suffer first, which could mean more distillers bottling their own product, and more clarity in the marketplace.

I asked Heaven Hill's CEO about the American whiskey shortage and he said, "If you order a whiskey anywhere in the world outside the United States, ninety-nine times out of a hundred, they will pour you a scotch. If just one more person got bourbon instead, every single distillery would sell out overnight."

"Well, between Scotch and nothin', I suppose I'd take Scotch. It's the nearest thing to good moonshine I can find."

—WILLIAM FAULKNER

CHAPTER FOUR

HOW TO MAKE WHISKEY

So, you want to break the law, or you would be skipping this chapter. This is fine, it's a good starting place, if perhaps a bit romanticized and bound to disappoint. While the crime is real and the punishment legitimate, they are abstractions that rarely come to bear on the home distiller. The wide gulf between the fact of the law and its enforcement is where you can build your career as a moonshiner. Really, what other reason is there to make whiskey? Few begin this endeavor to trim their monthly whiskey bill by bypassing the excise tax (you will not save money). Few are so dissatisfied with commercial whiskey that they insist on an alternative (though one can quite easily make a remarkably good one). Fewer still live in dry counties where there is no commercially available alcohol.

You are, perhaps, a tinkerer: mechanically inclined enough to believe you could build a still, which to your mind suggests that you should build a still, and that using that still to test your skill becomes an extension of the act of making it. Or perhaps you are a home brewer grown tired of that narrower art, hoping to add an element of distillation to your avocation and strike a definitive blow to your competitors in your local home-brew round robin. Maybe you are good in the kitchen, and have burned through your last cookbook. Or maybe you are simply rebellious by constitution, and you feel it is your right to make spirits.

But you would be wrong, in the sense that it is most certainly illegal to make spirituous alcohol in the United States and most other countries. What about for personal consumption? Isn't that legal? If you don't sell what you produce and only give it away? No, illegal. Simply owning an unlicensed still is a federal crime punishable by jail time. Americans may produce wine or beer at home, but may not boil alcohol so as to concentrate it into a spirit. A single drop of ethanol is forbidden.

Or so it is in the United States of America in 2013, and has been for 151 years. The excise tax on domestic spirits production accounts for only .16 of a percent of the $2.4 trillion U.S. revenue in 2012, and the volume of illegal moonshine confiscated is in the tens of thousands of gallons, cheating the government out of a few hundred thousand dollars each year at most. When the government was pulling in 65 percent of its income from excise tax in the late 1800s or even 20 percent in 1950, there was certainly more at stake. But a large moonshine raid of 100 gallons of illicit liquor these days accounts for lost revenue of about a week's wage for an administrative assistant in the bureau. The cost of enforcement now far outweighs the lost revenue, and chasing moonshiners is apparently something the government now invests in only on principle.

It's possible that the prohibition on home distillation will extend far into the twenty-first century, and bootleggers large and small, urban and rural, will always have to fear a knock on the door from the revenue service. On the other hand, as history suggests, America's relationship to spirits is never fixed—and can sometimes change dramatically, quickly. There's nothing categorically more sinful about making hard alcohol instead of soft. The only thing unsettling about thousands of our fellow citizens already making their own moonshine is that doing so makes them criminals. One could imagine an enterprising politician pointing out the illogic of this situation and getting some traction inviting moonshiners out from the shadow of law. But until that era arrives, this book is describing explicitly illegal activity. Which is all to say: You've been warned.

Before assembling your home distillery, take a moment and Google "distillery explosion." Distilling is dangerous. You should distill outside, if possible, or in a building that you wouldn't mind terribly if it burned down.

Fires and explosions occur when alcohol vapor comes into contact with an open flame or gathers at such intense pressure that it spontaneously combusts. A pot still is not a closed system, so it's difficult for pressure to build and become explosive, but it can and has happened at distilleries of every size. Two of the major distilleries in Kentucky have had fires in their recent history. A few years ago, five men operating an illegal still in Boston were killed in an explosion. Remember: Ventilation is important to dissipate any vapor that might escape. Never smoke or light candles near your still.

If you make the decision to distill in your home, avoid wood floors and plastic countertops in your work area, as the heat from the still can have an adverse affect, even if there is no fire. If you are using electricity to power your heat source, use an outlet that is connected to a GFCI circuit because water and electricity in close proximity can pose an electrocution hazard.

Finally, it is worth remembering that alcohol is a toxic substance, which is why we like it, but one of your responsibilities as a distiller is to separate the pleasantly toxic whiskey from the noxiously toxic by-products. This process is straightforward, and if conducted successfully your moonshine will contain fewer toxins than commercial vodka. Just make sure you don't skip the step of discarding the foreshots.

A NOTE ON HUBRIS

The first time I tried to fire up the still, it seemed a good opportunity to have a party. I invited several people to my apartment in Brooklyn, which had a secluded roof terrace situated between it and the adjacent apartment, enclosed on three sides by high walls. The terrace, which was really a stretch of tar paper with a drainpipe, had been decorated with a grill and some seats salvaged from Yankee Stadium. David, who had moved into the apartment before me, had set up an outdoor shower, which afforded access to cold water. The still was set up on a little wooden platform, and when the guests arrived, we hit the switch.

Beers were passed around, but visitors were warned to watch their consumption so as not to damage their palate or lessen their thirst for the nectar soon to drip from the still. An hour passed, then another. It was a chilly day for May, and we wondered if perhaps the wind was making it impossible for the still to maintain temperature. Time slowed; people yawned and drank more beer. At a certain point, the burgers were cooked and the still was basically abandoned as the party devolved. The kettle never came to a boil.

Two weeks later, after disassembling the cycling on the hotplate and installing some insulation around the kettle, we were distilling malt liquor into a noxious, putrid, high-proof solvent that seemed to qualify as moonshine. I was thrilled. Invariably, your first drop of moonshine will taste remarkable to you.

After a few more test runs, I was passing around some of this pernicious liquid at a friend's Fourth of July party, much to everyone's revulsion. I made few friends that day (and indeed was never invited back), but I felt proud. I had made moonshine, of sorts, and that was an accomplishment in itself. "Why can't you make it taste good?" someone asked. I thought about it and didn't have an answer.

I refined my recipe over weeks, then months. Online forums steered me wrong as often as they helped; trial and error seemed to be the only way to test for myself the impact of so many variables. I kept logs, and identified batches alphabetically with sequential first names that sounded Appalachian. I experimented with rye and wheat in addition to the usual mixtures of corn and barley, and drank a lot of my own whiskey trying to triangulate a flavor—and over time it happened. The whiskey tasted good. I still see people from that Fourth of July party, who probably think that Kings County whiskey must taste like that first malt-liquor moonshine. "How's *that* going for you?" they ask. Which brings us to a very important lesson: You get only one chance to make a first impression with your whiskey, so keep your circle small. It takes time to get something right, and to learn how the inputs and variables and constraints affect the output. Science is helpful but can be misleading, and sometimes you have no idea why something happens— why distillate is cloudy or tastes sulfuric, or why your mash has a low yield. There are any number of answers to each of these problems, and only time and commitment will help you find them.

Assembling Your Home Distillery

Most books on home distillation walk you through the process of building a still, and until not long ago this was a necessary rite of passage for the hobby distiller. If you were inexperienced in brazing copper, this was pretty much a deal breaker. However, the modern era has given us the Internet, and with it, the home-distillers'-supply website. At places like Mile Hi Distilling, Brewhaus, or Hillbilly Stills, you can let someone else braze copper so you can worry about distilling. There's no shame in buying a still, or maybe just a little, but not so much you can't make up for it.

The still is the only piece of specialty equipment necessary aside from a big stock pot, and is the most important decision in assembling the foundation of your home distillery. The configuration of the still will have a large impact on what you make. A chef is rarely judged by the type of stove he uses, but a distiller is somewhat at the mercy of what his still can produce.

A still is simply a pot or kettle with a heat source that is capable of boiling liquid and directing the vapor into a narrow column. The column sends the vapor over a bend into a condenser, or a pipe surrounded by cold water, and as it passes through, the vapor chills and condenses to droplets that run down a pipe or hose into a collection vessel. A pot still (or, more properly, an alembic still) is no more complicated than this. It is technically crude, and also inefficient, but it is the most traditional and common still for making moonshine. The goal is to turn liquid to vapor and condense it back down to liquid. Simple.

A more complex type of still, known as a reflux still, uses various mechanisms to encourage the vapor to condense and revaporize several times as it travels up the column from the kettle to the condenser arm. You may have seen the "professional" version of this sort of still on a distillery tour—machines with very tall columns and portholes

A small copper still built by Colonel Vaughn Wilson, a still manufacturer in Arkansas. This model offers two heads for more or less reflux.

that give the impression of a submarine on end. Many distillers prefer this type of still because it removes more impurities and it gives you a higher proof coming out of the still, which can seem like more of an achievement, and by extension, I suppose, more *awesome*.

Here we hit again upon that great divide in whiskey. Whiskey in the United States is defined by the proof at which it comes out of the still—it must be 80 percent alcohol or less—and this is a back-ended way of describing how the spirit is distilled. Recall that most vodka is made from similar grain mashes to whiskey, and the difference is that vodka is distilled for maximum purity and minimum taste. Vodka could be made in a pot still, but would have to be distilled many times over, and the reflux still eliminates that time and effort. American law allows whiskey to be produced in either, so long as the reflux still is adjusted to mimic the pot still. And so there is an argument for purchasing a reflux still: It is more flexible. On the other hand, it is more complicated to use, as it has more variables. You can make good whiskey in both types of still, but you'll have more flavor and a more traditional whiskey distilling twice with a pot still. Chris Morris, the master distiller at

Woodford Reserve, one of the few Kentucky distilleries to use pot stills, described the distinction to me this way: "A column still produces a lighter bodied, crisper spirit, and pot stills make heavier bodied, more textured spirit."

For centuries, copper has been the material of choice in still construction, and nearly all professional stills are built from or lined with copper. Copper removes certain sulfuric compounds from the distillate and thus can yield a cleaner-tasting whiskey. But it's my personal opinion that copper is not explicitly necessary and there are other variables that will have a much greater influence on the end product. Many stills sold online are built from steel, and you can easily line the inside of your column with sheets of copper to get the same effect as a copper still, with less trouble and expense.

HEAT SOURCE

Some hobby stills come with a heat source; others are built to sit on top of a stove or hotplate. If you are purchasing one without a heat source, be advised that most commonly available hotplates that run on 110 current will have trouble boiling six gallons of mash, so you might look for a more industrial model from a restaurant supply store. Another option is a magnetic-induction hotplate, which is more efficient and can boil faster, but it doesn't work with every still (the boiler must be made from a grade of steel that works with induction plates). You can also use direct flame from a gas stove, a propane burner, or a wood fire. However, as mentioned in the note about safety, it's never a great idea to have an open flame near alcohol vapor, so use utmost caution—and certainly work outside—if you decide to go this route.

CONDENSER

Since distilling requires cooling and heating in the same device, you will need a source of cold water for the condenser. Many distillers can hook their stills up to a sink and run tap water through the condenser, but this is very wasteful (and potentially costly if you pay for your water)

The graduated cylinder, distiller's hydrometer (with proof or tralles scale), and thermometer are a distiller's essential scientific tools.

and you can get good results with a reservoir made from a plastic cooler, bucket, or your bathtub and an aquarium pump. If the temperature gets above 90°F (32°C), you'll have to empty and refresh your reservoir, but you will ultimately use a small fraction of the water you would use with the tap constantly flowing. It is said that a consistently cool condenser (65°F/18°C or less) has advantages in terms of yield and flavor on the whiskey, but I've never noticed a difference in yield or taste on our setup. It's your call.

THERMOMETER

It's very important to have a dependable thermometer, and I like to have a couple of different types around. Even lab-grade thermometers tend to be unreliable or break at a key moment. I suggest a digital-readout meat thermometer, and a glass brewer's thermometer as a backup. Finding a reliable thermometer is hard, so when you do, try not to break it. Some digital thermometers come with alarms that you can program to particular temperatures. This is helpful as a reminder to turn on your condenser and pay attention to the still.

HYDROMETER

A distiller's hydrometer, or an "alcoholometer," is necessary. A hydrometer is a weighted glass bobber that floats in a liquid and measures its density with a calibrated scale along its stem. A distiller's hydrometer is designed to read percent alcohol by volume (abv), or sometimes percent proof, in a mixture of pure water and ethanol. Percent proof is double percent alcohol, so a spirit at 50 percent abv will be 100 proof, a common benchmark for a spirit's quality in the 1800s. Bacardi 151, named after its proof, is 75.5 percent alcohol. Percent abv is also called the tralles scale, so a proof and tralles hydrometer will just read 1–100 on one side and 1–200 on the other. A good glass test tube is also required to use the hydrometer, and a 150 ml to 250 ml graduated cylinder can be used with most. A brewer's hydrometer may also be useful but is not necessary. It measures the specific gravity of liquids denser than water and is used to calculate how much potential alcohol you can get from your mash.

OTHER EQUIPMENT

You will need a 10-gallon (38-L) stock pot, a 10-gallon (38-L) plastic fermenting bucket, a wide-mesh laundry bag, a dozen mason jars, and two glass 1-gallon (4-L) jugs. Whiskey should be stored in glass, as high-proof alcohol can cause certain plastics to leach chemicals. (If you must purchase anything plastic that will come in contact with high-proof spirit, check with a distillery supply site and ensure that it is chemical tolerant.) A log book is helpful to record the details of your distillations.

THE INGREDIENTS

The following recipe is for Kings County Distillery's corn whiskey, and the process described here follows very precisely the one we used in our first two years of operation, when we distilled on 8-gallon (30-L) hobby stills. This is the recipe we followed every day; it is one of the most classic moonshine recipes you will find. It does not include sugar, which is a staple of post-Prohibition Southern moonshine but is also a

Most brewery-supply stores sell grains useful to the distiller, but you can also buy unprocessed grains directly from local farms.

cheat. Nor does it call for rye or wheat, two grains that often show up on the mash bill of American whiskeys. Better to start simply, and once your corn whiskey is strong, begin to improvise with alterations and additions. This basic recipe and summary of procedures owes a great debt to Ian Smiley and his *Making Pure Corn Whiskey*. The book takes a different view of certain aspects of distillation, but remains the most indispensable resource to a home whiskey distiller.

Corn whiskey has only three essential ingredients: corn, malted barley, and yeast. Many home distillers recommend using flaked maize as a base grain. This is corn that has been steamed and flatted in a process similar to the one used in making oatmeal (which, incidentally, you can also distill). Flaked maize is used by home brewers who want to include corn in their beer, and is sold at home-brew shops. Unfortunately, the corn is heavily processed and not especially flavorful, and I recommend instead that you call a farm and purchase cracked corn directly from them. Cracked corn is more coarsely ground and is commonly used as animal feed. It takes longer to mash, but I find you extract better flavor from corn that is closer to whole kernel.

The barley that we use at Kings County has been malted, which means the seeds have been allowed to germinate slightly, and then the seeds are dried in a kiln before they begin to sprout. The word *malt* generally refers to malted barley, though any grain can be malted, which causes some confusion. The malted grain has a different enzyme profile than a dormant grain—the same enzymes a plant uses to convert its stored starch into energy are used by distillers to convert the starch from corn into sugar, which the yeast then converts into alcohol.

You should buy dedicated whiskey yeast from a home-brew supply store or online distiller's supply store. There are many different yeasts available, and in my experience, only yeast that has been cultivated to work with the types of fermentable sugars in the common whiskey grains is best. In many cases, the yeast will come packaged with amyloglucosidase (AG), an enzyme that aids the malt enzymes in breaking down the starch in the corn.

OTHER INGREDIENTS

Some distillers will try to justify the use of a number of additives, such as gypsum powders, pH adjusters, powdered enzymes, and yeast nutrients, which are all offered at home-brew shops. While they may boost your yield, they will add needless variables to your process and should be considered optional at best.

Step 1: Mashing

Mashing is a complicated process, and if you're distilling for the first time, I suggest skipping this step, buying a jug of table wine or a bottle of malt liquor, and throwing that into the still. Sometimes it's easier to start with distilling and work backward, mashing only when you are confident that you can successfully distill the alcohol that you've gone through the trouble to make yourself.

If you are a home brewer and already know how to make alcohol from grain, then I would also suggest that you skip this step; your first distillation attempts will be largely experimental and you don't want to waste good beer. However, this is a great opportunity to get rid of a batch that you weren't in love with. (Note that whiskey does not generally involve hops, so if you are distilling beer, the less-hopped versions will make more-familiar-tasting whiskey.)

BASIC CORN WHISKEY

For those who are ready to make whiskey from grain to bottle, the recipe goes like this:

6 gallons (23 L) water
8 quarts (7.5 L) cracked corn
2 quarts (1.9 L) crushed malted barley
1 single-use packet (5 g) whiskey yeast

Heat the water in your 10-gallon (38-L) stockpot. When it boils, remove from heat. Add the cracked corn and stir. Cover the mash and let sit for an hour, stirring every 15 minutes. The goal here is to disperse the starch in the liquid, so you are breaking down the corn as much as possible. Remove the lid and wait for the mash to cool to 155°F (68°C) throughout (stir thoroughly to get a consistent temperature—the mash can be thick and hold pockets of heat). Then add the crushed malted barley. You'll notice that the mash will thin and become sweeter very quickly. Stir and cover for 45 minutes. After this step, your mash will

Measure 8 quarts (7.5 L) of cracked corn.

taste almost as if you've added white sugar, though it is just the malt acting to convert the corn starch and malt to their composite sugars. Over time, you can gauge the success of your starch conversion by taste.

Stir the mash again and leave it to cool to room temperature for 6 to 8 hours. Note that mash that is left unattended for more than 8 hours is susceptible to lactobacillus infection. You will know it if it happens: There will be a white, filmy substance that looks somewhat powdery, and an overpowering smell of rot and decay. Successful mash should smell like grassy popcorn. Throw away any infected mash and start again.

If you find yourself plagued with chronic bacterial infection, you can cool the mash more quickly by using a wort chiller, which is a copper coil that runs cold water through the mash. In most indoor environments, this shouldn't be necessary, but anything can happen. (After Hurricane Irene, all our mash got infected with lactobacillus. We are not sure why—maybe the wind carried more microorganisms than normal—but it took us more than a week to recover.)

Add the cracked corn to boiling water, turn off the heat,
and let stand for an hour, stirring every 15 minutes.

Once the mash is cooled to room temperature (or a little
above), you can check the specific gravity (or density) of your mash
with a brewer's hydrometer. Fill a test tube full of the clear liquid on
top of your mash and sink the hydrometer. The thicker the liquid, the
more sugar you have in your mash, and the more potential alcohol the
yeast can make. However, at this point, what's done is done, and this
measurement is helpful only in terms of guiding your next batch, so
record the reading in your log book.

Next, add the yeast. Yeast require oxygen, and the boiling step
removes it, so you must add it back by aerating your mash. You can do
this by stirring it aggressively for a few minutes or pouring the mash
from one bucket to another back and forth four times.

Most yeast comes in single-use packets for this size mash, with
instructions that you should follow. It may need to be jumpstarted in
warm water, but most likely you can sprinkle a packet on the top of your
mash. Make sure you are using whiskey yeast and not "turbo yeast,"
which is designed for sugar washes. Transfer the mash into a covered, but
not fully sealed, container and place it somewhere that won't get cold.

Leave the yeasted mash to ferment.

Step 2: Fermenting

This is the easy part. You can pretty much let your mash sit for a few days and read a book or drink some whiskey. Generally, fermentation lasts somewhere from three to five days and ends when the bubbling slows considerably (it will keep bubbling for a long time, but when the bubbles slow, you are winding down; letting the mash sit too long will leave it susceptible to other bacterial infections).

You don't have to stir, although you may want to, as it causes the yeast to bubble and makes you feel like you are participating in the process. If the mash gets too thick, the yeast may get trapped and run out of nutrients. If the mash gets too cold, you will see a decrease in yield. I have been told that allowing the temperature to rise above 90°F (32°C) will kill the yeast, but we have also run our distillery through three very hot New York summers, without air conditioning, and never encountered a problem. It depends almost entirely on the yeast.

Using a mesh laundry bag, strain out the solid grains and add them to your compost.

Step 3: Straining

When the fermentation has slowed, and you are ready to distill, you will want to strain out the solids that are left in the mash. There is no good way to do this, but a wide-gauge nylon laundry bag is a starting place. If you cut a hole in the base of a 5-gallon (19-L) bucket, you can place it on a chair such that the liquid drains into a collection container. If your stockpot is handy, that can work to collect the liquid, or you can directly load your still kettle. Put the laundry bag in the bucket as if it is a garbage bag, and tighten the cord so it won't slip off. As you pour your mash into the bucket, much of it will drain out on its own. After a while, the draining will slow, and you can tighten the cord in the laundry bag and gradually squeeze out as much of the liquid as you have patience for. The leftover corn should be spongy and moist, but not gloppy. Keep this corn separate and use it as fertilizer, animal feed, or muffin mix. One home distiller cooks his spent grain into Hillbilly Bread (for the full recipe, see Chapter Five).

Load the still with the fermented wash, now strained of solids.
You can siphon it into the still using a plastic hose to minimize mess.

Step 4: The Stripping Run

Because the pot still is a crude mechanism for distillation, the alcohol that comes out of the still during this phase is not yet palatable. Too many fusel oils and other impurities make it through the distillation, and the distillate, at this point known as low wines, will be cloudy and noxious. That's fine. The idea here is to run the still to "strip" out all the alcohol, reducing the liquid to about a third of its original volume, and you are not yet concerned about flavor.

Pour the yellow mash (which, now that it is strained, is properly called a wash) into the still. Assemble the still and turn the heat to its maximum level. The still will take at least an hour to heat up. After an hour or two, the temperature in the column will spike. If you have a thermometer with an alarm, set it for 150°F (65°C). If your thermometer doesn't have an alarm, you can fix a soda can to your column with a bit of paraffin or beeswax. When the can clanks to the floor, it's time to head to the still and pay attention.

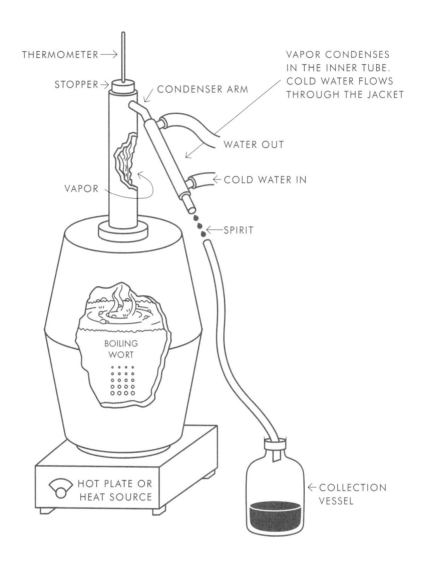

THERMOMETER →

STOPPER →

CONDENSER ARM

VAPOR CONDENSES
IN THE INNER TUBE.
COLD WATER FLOWS
THROUGH THE JACKET

WATER OUT

← COLD WATER IN

VAPOR

← SPIRIT

BOILING
WORT

HOT PLATE OR
HEAT SOURCE

← COLLECTION
VESSEL

HOW A STILL WORKS

This diagram shows a consumer, or hobbyist, still, much like those available from
Brewhaus, Mile Hi Distilling, or Hillbilly Stills. This particular still is configured
to operate like a pot still, with no packing in the column and no condenser water
running through the top of the still, which is known as a dephlegmator or
pre-condenser. The condenser is a shell-and-tube heat exchanger that can be run
on tap water or with a reservoir and aquarium pump. This setup uses a hot plate,
but some stills have heating elements built in.

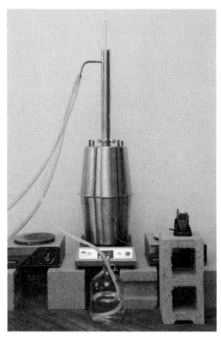

Collect 1 to 1⅓ gallons of low wines during your stripping run.

When the temperature reaches 150°F (65°C), turn on your condenser. Remember that alcohol boils at a lower temperature than water, so it is important not to miss gathering the very first liquid. If you see steam emerging from your still, that's another signal to turn on the condenser, but catch it before then, as it is not only dangerous to have high-proof vapor emerging from your still, but you'll also be losing the most productive part of the run. Once the cold water is running though your condenser, you may have a few minutes until the still starts dripping. Place a gallon jug below the condenser to collect the liquid. The still will begin dripping at about 170°F (77°C). Reduce the heat by half, so as to prevent burning and extend your run. Most distillers believe that a longer, extended distillation makes for a smoother spirit, as there will be more natural reflux in the column that will soften it.

TESTING THE PROOF

It's not necessary, but you may want to test the proof while your still is stripping. Collect 150 ml (about 5 ounces) in a graduated cylinder and sink in your distiller's hydrometer. It should float. Read the proof

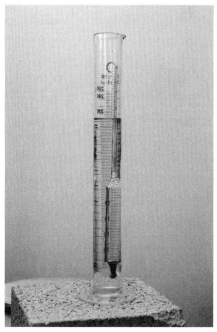

Use a hydrometer to measure the proof of your low wines.

at the meniscus and you will have a general idea of the alcohol content, but to get a truly accurate reading, you must temperature-correct the measurement. Most hydrometers are calibrated to read at 60°F/15°C (it must be assumed you are distilling in a cave), and if the distillate approaches 90°F (32°C), the proof can be as much as 6 percent lower than the hydrometer reads. Take the temperature with your best thermometer and write down both numbers. To derive the true proof from the apparent proof, download the chart that the federal government provides to distillers: "The True Percents of Proof Spirit for Any Indication of the Hydrometer at Temperatures Between 0° and 100°." It was created October 15, 1913. It's very handy.

Your stripping run will start dripping at a high proof, and the alcohol percentage will quickly taper off and then gradually run down to zero as you approach the boiling point of water. The rule of thumb is to distill until the percent alcohol of what's coming out of the still matches what you put into the still. Your 1–100 percent distiller's hydrometer may not be that reliable at lower proofs, but don't worry too much. If you shut it off too soon, you'll lose a very small percentage of

Load the low wines into the still to begin the spirit run. This run must be monitored more closely, as it is the part of the process during which you determine what of the spirit you will drink, recycle, and discard.

your alcohol; if you shut it off too late, you'll have wasted some time and energy boiling off water. Neither is a catastrophe. The stripping run should take 6 to 7 hours, but it depends entirely on your heat source and how fast you run your still. At the end of this process, you will have 1 to 1.3 gallons (3.8 to 4.9 L) of low wines.

After your run is complete, turn off the heat and let the condenser run for a few minutes to extract the remaining vapor. Turn off the condenser and let your still cool. When it's cool enough to handle, disassemble the still and clean it carefully.

Step 5: The Spirit Run

The spirit run is the most critical step of the distillation process, as decisions now have the greatest impact on your whiskey. While the stripping run must occur soon after the fermentation is complete, the spirit run can take place anytime—your low wines will never go bad (and it may be mildly beneficial to rest them). Begin the spirit run as you began the stripping run, but instead of filling the still with your wash, you should now load the still with the collected low wines. For your first few runs, it may be helpful to add a gallon of water, as this can stretch out your run and extend the time you have to make cuts.

Assemble the still and turn the heat to maximum. Set an alarm for 150°F (65°C) so you can turn on the condenser well before you start to see vapor. Once you turn on the condenser, you must wait patiently for the first drips to appear. Have a graduated cylinder poised under the spirit outlet to collect anything you miss should your attention wander.

MAKING THE CUTS

The still will create a steady drip of spirit starting around 168°F (75°C) and will continue until the temperature climbs to 212°F (100°C) and you are distilling only water. Throughout this run, you will be determining which parts get set aside for consumption, what gets recycled, and what should be thrown away.

Ethanol, the type of alcohol we drink, boils at 173°F (78°C). Whiskey, however, is more than just ethanol; it is a mixture of pure ethanol (the sole ingredient in neutral grain spirit), trace chemicals that boil at a lower temperature than ethanol, and esters and "fusel oils," or longer-chain alcohol molecules that boil at higher temperatures. Together these impurities are referred to as congeners, and they are what give whiskey its flavor.

The key congeners in whiskey include: acetaldehyde, acetone, ethyl acetate, methanol, propanol, isobutanol, and amyl alcohol. Some of these are toxic; some are harmless. Methanol, for instance, is extremely toxic, and drinking it pure will quickly cause dizziness and confusion. Even 10 ml can cause blindness and as little as 30 ml can be fatal. The presence of methanol in any given batch of moonshine will be much less than this (a fraction of a milliliter), but proper distillation is required to regulate the amount and type of methanol and other congeners that make it through to the whiskey.

The mechanism for doing so is called making cuts, or separating the spirit run into distinct phases. All whiskey will contain some of the congeners from the front and back of the run, but it takes time to learn how to get the balance correct. And also to learn what you like. I know a rye distiller who only collected about a quart of whiskey from her 8 gallons of mash (by taking only the spirit coming off 75 to 70 percent). It was incredibly smooth and nearly perfect, but very labor intensive.

The four phases of the whiskey spirit distillation are known as foreshots, heads, hearts, and tails. These phases are essentially arbitrary: There is no true "heart" of the run; it is merely a judgment based on preference, taste, and tradition. For professional distillers, it is easiest to make distinctions between these phases by monitoring the proof of the spirit as it comes out of the still and making a judgment based on smell and/or taste. The "cut" is achieved by switching collection vessels, cutting off one phase, and moving to another. The volume of spirit produced by a hobby distiller, however, affords an opportunity that professional distillers don't conveniently have: to collect the spirit in small samples during the duration of the run, and make the cuts after the fact by evaluating each sample independently.

Before your spirit still reaches 150°F (65°C), label your mason jars one through sixteen. Line them in a row, and once distillate begins to come off the still, gather 150 ml in each. Note the time you begin each jar and the temperature at the top of the still's column. Test the proof of each jar as it is filled (you can measure the volume and proof of the sample in a graduated cylinder before emptying it into the jar). This information will be useful as you distill more regularly and learn to cross-reference your proof measurements with other methods of tracking the course of the run, like time and temperature.

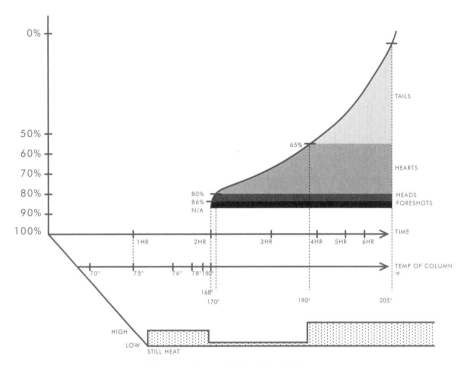

GRAPH OF A DISTILLATION RUN

Over the course of the spirit run (or second distillation), the temperature rises and the distillate coming off of the still changes. The still will start dripping sometime between one hour and two hours into the run, often around 170°F. The emerging distillate will start at a very high proof and then will gradually taper down during the course of the run. The chart shows approximately where to make foreshots, heads, hearts, and tails cuts, but every still operates differently, and this should be up to the distiller's judgment. It is best to make a narrow hearts cut when learning and expand with subsequent runs.

Once you have filled all your jars, the spirit run will have squarely reached the tails. You can now turn up the heat on the still until you have filled 1½ gallons (5.68 L) of tails, or until the still is producing less than 5 percent alcohol (again, the hydrometer may not be very accurate, so err on the side of taking too much). During this phase, you don't need to monitor the still as closely, but keep an eye on things so that your condenser water stays cold and your jug doesn't overflow.

When the run is finished, turn off the heat and let the condenser run for a few minutes to get all the steam into the column that is possible. Turn the condenser off and disassemble and clean your still.

Once you have your jars lined up, you can begin to evaluate them. The first jar will contain the foreshots: a noxious clear cocktail of the majority of congeners (and toxins) that would potentially cause

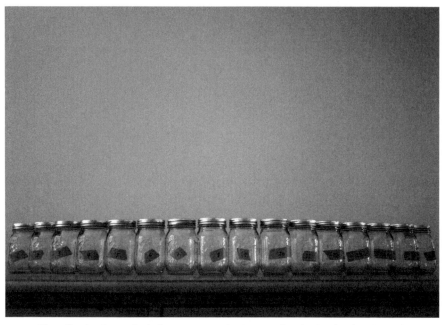

The collection-jar method allows you to make the cuts after the fact by choosing only the jars you feel will yield the best whiskey.

your whiskey to do more damage than intended, and will certainly be detrimental to its taste and smell. Keep your foreshots separated and clearly labeled in a jar or jug labeled with "XXX." It's a conversation piece and a helpful cleaning agent, but nothing you want to consume.

The following one or two jars will contain the heads. The general rule is that everything after the foreshots and above 80 percent alcohol is considered heads (this is based on the legal definition of whiskey, which mandates taking hearts starting at 80 percent or below). However, each still will run differently and proof is not universally reliable, so taste and smell should be your guide. You want to get past the solvent-like, nail-polish-remover phase of the run, and anything after foreshots that still smells or tastes harsh should be considered heads. If your fermentation is weak, you may find that you don't have heads at all, and that jar number two smells fine. In this case, you can move directly to the hearts. In my experience, you will find heads in about equal quantity to the foreshots, but it's really a judgment. I find that I prefer a more heads-side whiskey, so my heads are quite limited, while in Scotland they only start collecting hearts at 75 percent. It really depends on the still, the whiskey, and its maker.

Jars three through twelve will likely contain the hearts, which is the part that you will want to call your whiskey. Hearts usually run from 80 to 75 percent down to 65 to 55 percent as measured by the hydrometer. Smell and taste each jar: You will find the aroma of the heads mellow out into a very rich, bright whiskey smell. The distillate will be clear and viscous. Somewhere around jar ten, the aroma will develop a more pungent smell, like NutraSweet, skunky beer, or unused baby diapers. This signals the end of the hearts. Most professional distillers run their stills down to 55 percent, but most home distillers, less financially incentivized to stretch the size of their run, may want to stop in the mid-60s. The narrower the run, generally speaking, the better the whiskey, so start with narrow cuts and work your way out.

It is important to continue your spirit distillation beyond the hearts and into the tails. While the tails aren't pure enough to drink, they have plenty of ethanol that can be useful for subsequent runs. After you start distilling repeatedly, you will want to recycle the heads and tails of the previous spirit run into the next one—they will help maximize yields of future runs and maintain a consistent flavor from batch to batch. If you find your flavor profile veering away from what you like, you can discard the heads and tails and start over from scratch.

The collection-jar method described here is laborious, and after you've done it a few times, you will want to reduce the number of collection vessels to three: for foreshots, for the "feints" (the combined heads and tails), and for hearts. You will still want to collect samples at various times throughout the run, measuring with a hydrometer, cross-referencing it to the still-head thermometer, and gut checking with your nose. The nose tends to be more reliable than the tongue, since alcohol percentage can have a dramatic impact on flavor, and it is difficult to compare two samples of different proof. On the other hand, taste is the ultimate arbiter and scent can occasionally be deceptive. The best way to taste a sample of what is coming off the still is to dilute it to 30 to 40 percent. (Higher proofs will kill all the bacteria in your mouth, impairing your taste buds for the rest of the process.) And never sample foreshots, even for curiosity's sake.

Most distillers will want to cut their whiskey down to a more palatable proof.
Anything from 40 to 50 percent abv is standard.

Step 6: Proofing

Whether you use the collection-jar method or the conventional method, at the end of your spirit distillation you will have about 1 to 2.5 quarts (1 to 2.5 liters) of hearts at around 70 percent abv or slightly higher.

The next step is to dilute your whiskey to drinking strength. All commercially sold alcohol has been diluted with water after coming off the still. Most whiskeys are bottled between 40 percent and 50 percent abv. It seems a little silly to spend all this effort separating the alcohol from water, only to dilute it back with more water, but distilling is as much about removing impurities as it is about isolating alcohol.

For moonshine, or any unaged spirit, I recommend 40 percent abv (80 proof) as a standard starting point. Assuming you and your friends will be drinking the whiskey neat, this will highlight your work, and not let the heat of the alcohol overwhelm the taste of the spirit. But if you anticipate serving it on the rocks, or using it in a complicated cocktail, you should consider a higher proof. Similarly, aged and infused whiskeys are mellower than naked ones, and can handle an alcohol percentage of 45 to 50.

Be sure to use bottled distilled water from the grocery store—not tap water—for your dilution. At this point, your whiskey is perfect, and you don't want to corrupt it with minerals and fluoride. To dilute, gradually add water to your jug of hearts until the hydrometer reads the desired proof. Sometimes it's helpful to adjust for temperature in advance, so you know the target for the anticipated temperature of your sample. For example, if you are diluting a sample that is 70°F (21°C) to 40 percent abv, you will want to aim for a hydrometer reading a touch over 42 percent. And if you over-dilute, you'll have to have some extra spirit on hand to correct.

Proofing is always a confusing step, as it's hard to remember whether the reading is indicating that you have more or less alcohol than you think. Just remember that alcohol expands when it gets warmer, therefore becoming less dense, and so the hydrometer will sink lower in the cylinder, making you think you have more booze than you really do. Learn to use the chart.

As you dilute, you may note that around 45 percent abv, your spirit becomes cloudy. This is normal. It is called a "louche," and it occurs because certain whiskey impurities are alcohol-soluble but not water-soluble. Absinthe, ouzo, and some other high-ester spirits experience the same effect. In cold temperatures, the oils may congeal in what will appear as little white clouds in your container, but these will mostly dissipate upon shaking. Other than perhaps being unsightly, there is nothing wrong with a cloudy spirit. Nearly all commercial whiskeys are chill-filtered to remove these oils, but many home distillers prefer to keep them. In fact, this is one of the biggest benefits to making your own whiskey, as the mouth-feel of unfiltered whiskey is much better than that of chill-filtered whiskey. Removing the louche thins out flavor, and some smaller microdistilleries (including ours) would prefer instead to educate the customer on its benefits.

There's no substitute for the mellowing effects of barrel aging your whiskey. Small barrels of a size suitable for the home distiller are available online and are a nice way to add dimension to your whiskey.

Step 7: Aging

White whiskey, while common in the nineteenth century, endured a bad reputation for the duration of the twentieth. Bourbon and rye (and the variant of bourbon known as Tennessee whiskey) dominated the category to the exclusion of nearly all other types of whiskey. While white or unaged tequilas, rums, and brandies exist on equal footing with their aged counterparts, white whiskey was deemed undrinkable, perhaps because of the negative associations with Prohibition moonshine.

If you've made good cuts, it is unlikely that you'll need to age your whiskey. But your constituency may desire it. Moonshine, while gaining in acceptance, still has a stigma. And it's also very gratifying to age whiskey, to observe the spirit transform from the beneficial mellowing effects of wood.

Properly aging a whiskey requires a barrel. There's no real substitute for the way changes in pressure inside the barrel send the whiskey through the pores of the charred wood as the volatile compounds in the distillate break down or evaporate over time. The charred wood both filters impurities out of the whiskey (chemicals that may have slipped past your heads cut, and esters that may have seeped in before your tails cut) and infuses the whiskey with the sap and caramelized sugars of the tree wood.

Aging whiskey is governed by a number of conditions. Barrel size determines what percentage of spirit comes in contact with the wood. Char level indicates how deeply the wood has been burned inside, and will affect the speed of aging and the flavor of the spirit. Changes in temperature (and especially periods of extreme heat) will speed the aging process, as changes in temperature outside the barrel correlate to changes in pressure inside. Some distillers even argue for vibrating or agitating the barrels to ensure that the infusion of flavors is dispersed frequently, though this has less effect than a cycle of heating and cooling.

Small barrels (½- to 3-gallon [2 to 11-L] size) are available from a number of specialty coopers and are sometimes sold at home-brew shops. They are ideal for the home distiller. Because there is much more surface area relative to the amount of liquid inside, whiskey in these barrels ages more quickly than commercial whiskey stored in large barrels (months versus years). If there is an option for a lighter toast, you can usually extend the aging process to something that will sound respectable when you are inevitably asked. Keep the barrel near a heat source if you want it to age quickly, or a cool or temperate place if you opt for a slower aging process.

If you cannot locate a barrel, you can experiment with toasted woodchips instead. While they won't do as good a job filtering out impurities, they will infuse and color the spirit with the familiar oak profile. (Tennessee whiskey gets its characteristic wood-heavy character from a bath in charred maple chips before entering the barrel.) It's not a bad idea to age your first few batches of corn whiskey using oak chips, so you have a rough sense of what the barrel-aged bourbon will taste like.

How will you know when your whiskey is "mature"? This is a fairly loaded question, and the easy answer is that it's mature when you like it. One suggestion: Put three jars of the same spirit away on woodchips and pull them at predetermined times, one month apart. Generally, I find that people prefer more wood than less. I sometimes disparagingly compare the contribution of the barrel to salt: It's familiar, it usually enhances flavor, and people can't seem to get enough, even after it throws off the balance of the whiskey. But remember, longer aging does not always make things better. Every whiskey has a sweet spot: Before the whiskey is mature, the taste will be like wet lumber, not quite complex. When the barrel reaches its peak, the taste will have notes of vanilla and caramel from sugars and, depending on your methods, spicy notes of cinnamon, nutmeg, and black pepper. This is what we look for when we pull barrels. An over-aged barrel will become heavy and leathery and taste exclusively of campfire, and the spicy notes will become dampened.

Proof makes a difference, too. According to U.S. law, bourbon and other American whiskeys must be barreled at less than 62.5 percent alcohol. Higher proof during aging extracts more alcohol-soluble flavors, while lower proof extracts more water-soluble flavors. I find that with our whiskey, the lower-proof barrels extract more sweet, floral notes, while the higher-proof barrels tend to have more spicy notes. In our early days, I asked the former master distiller of Glenmorangie what proof he recommended we barrel our whiskey, and he suggested barreling a single batch at multiple proofs and picking what we liked best. It was a diplomatic answer, but also honest and an acknowledgment that there are rarely right answers or even fixed principles for all whiskeys. I asked the same question of the folks at Heaven Hill, and they said, "The law lets you fit up to 125 proof, and barrels are expensive." Indeed, nearly all Kentucky distilleries enter their spirit into the barrel at the legal maximum.

Other Recipes

Once you've mastered the basic corn whiskey, you might want to move on to rye, bourbon, wheat, scotch-style malt whiskey, or other spirits like rum or brandy. Here are some recipes to get you thinking about other types of whiskeys and spirits.

SOUR MASH

Many people use this phrase synonymously with bourbon, and most large Kentucky distilleries do use a sour mash process, though most smaller distilleries don't. After a stripping run, the liquid left in the still is called the backset. If you make a new mash using some of this backset, it's called a sour mash. In principle, the acid-rich backset creates ideal conditions for the yeast. The alternative is sometimes called a sweet mash recipe, which is most common among home distillers who are trying a lot of different recipes, but if you are trying to repeat the same one with greatest efficiency, you might try adopting a sour mash recipe.

To make a sour mash corn whiskey, take 1.5 gallons (5.68 L) out of what is leftover in your still after the stripping run and, instead of running it down the drain or into a garden, pour it into your mash pot and mix with 4.5 gallons (17 L) of water. Begin the Basic Corn Whiskey recipe from this point on, and you'll have a sour mash corn whiskey.

CLASSIC BOURBON

Classic bourbon recipes use a sour mash process and include some rye as a flavor grain. Mix 6 quarts (5.7 L) of corn and 2 quarts (1.9 L) of ground rye or rye flour into the boiling water right after you remove it from the heat. Add the barley at 155°F (68°C) as if you were following the Basic Corn Whiskey recipe. The resulting mash will have a grassier, rounded flavor that will be familiar to bourbon drinkers.

KITCHEN MOONSHINE

This is the most common moonshine recipe around, made with items that can be found around the kitchen. In the largest saucepan or stockpot you have, bring 1 gallon (3.8 L) of water to a boil. Mix in 1 quart (.9 L) cornmeal and 1 tablespoon wheat germ. Turn off the heat and stir until the liquid cools to about 100°F (37°C). Add in 4 pounds (1.8 kg) white sugar until dissolved. Add 4 gallons (15 L) of room-temperature water and mix thoroughly. Add 2 packets of baker's yeast and allow to ferment. Distill as with the other recipes. In this case, the corn is merely there for flavor, so you can adjust the recipe as you like (or use other grain substitutions).

SUGAR-WASH MOONSHINE

This is the easiest recipe to make. Go to a home-brew supply store and buy something called "turbo yeast." Then go to the grocery store and buy three 5-pound (2-kg) bags of white sugar, or read the recipe on the back of the yeast for what they recommend. This type of yeast is designed to work only with sugar, needs no further additives or nutrients, and will give high yields during the fermentation in a short amount of time. The resulting spirit is technically rum, though not a very delicate one.

SINGLE MALT WHISKEY

Malt whiskey is fairly easy to make, as home-brew shops carry a variety of malts, though beware as some specialty malts (chocolate malts and roasted malts) often no longer have the enzymes that are necessary for starch conversion. For a true, scotch-style malt whiskey, you should find a peated barley malt. Some of these are more heavily peated than others; I like to mix half peated malt with our regular malt and go from there.

Heat 6 gallons (23 L) of water to 155°F (68°C), add 6 quarts (5.7 L) peated malt and 6 quarts (5.7 L) barley malt, stir periodically for about an hour as the enzymes work, and then follow the directions for Basic Corn Whiskey from there. A red scotch distillery will strain out the solids before the fermentation, though this isn't necessary, and it's easier to strain at the end when the mash is thinner. This uses a little more grain than the other recipes, but will give a better yield.

BRANDY

Brandy is really any spirit distilled from fermented fruit juice, though the most common type of brandy is from fermented grape juice (also known as wine). There are many types of grape brandy, but perhaps the best known is cognac, a protected classification of brandy from that region of France. Making wine is its own subject, but home winemakers are pretty easy to find, and could provide you with a carboy or two to run off, provided you share the spoils. Peach wine, pear wine, and apple cider all make interesting spirit, and even more interesting with a little oak added through chips or a small barrel.

Kings County Distillery started out in a 325-square-foot room on the second floor of a warehouse. Starting small is a good way to work out recipes and legal issues before you sink too much time and money.

Starting a Distillery

So you've been moonshining for a while and you are making whiskey you like, maybe even whiskey you find distinctive, and you are doing so with enough confidence that it has occurred to you that you might want to quit your day job. Maybe you aren't making a whole lot of whiskey, but you are designing your bottle and coming up with T-shirts and taglines for the whiskey that you might make if you were more persistent about running the still. You are talking to a rich uncle about bankrolling the operation and scouring Craigslist for real estate opportunities.

To sell alcohol, you need a couple of key things: a federal license to cover your distillery, issued by the TTB, and a state license. You may also need to file with the local or city government, depending on the jurisdiction. You will need a lease on a commercial space (you cannot receive a distilled spirits plant [DSP] permit in or on the property of a dwelling), and you will need to raise some money to pay for a lawyer, a bond, equipment, and a down payment on your commercial lease.

The federal permit is free, though filing it is complicated and collecting the information is important. Every investor holding at least 10 percent of your company must fill out a questionnaire, and you must file your lease or deed to the property where you intend to distill; detailed floor plans; a listing of equipment, with serial numbers; and detailed security measures. The federal license takes from two to six months to obtain.

After you are licensed to make alcohol, you still need to bottle it, and the feds closely monitor how spirits are labeled. A Certificate of Label Approval (COLA) is required for all spirits you produce. Some spirits also require a formula approval if the product you produce falls outside of the very basic categories of whiskey, vodka, gin, and a few others.

Most states now have provisions for small distilleries, but they differ in what advantages they afford entrepreneurs. In New York State, Kings County Distillery holds a "farm distillery" license, which is a variant of the small distillers license that allows for a tasting room but mandates ingredients sourced from in-state farms. It also has a provision for self-distribution, which is an advantage. (We do all of our deliveries ourselves.)

Our state license took six months from the date we filed to get approval. The state also required detailed floor plans as well as an area survey to prove that the distillery was not located near a church or a school. Some states require community-board approval for alcohol-related establishments, which can require some diplomacy to help the community to adjust to the idea. Like the feds, most states also require brand approval or registration with the state, which may also include listing prices in advance.

Once you have settled on a commercial space, you will need to ensure that the space complies with local codes for manufacturing, which may mean getting a revised Certificate of Occupancy or other certifications. While alcohol is not considered food (which allows distillers to avoid the health regulations of restaurants and other food facilities), your space should still comply with food-manufacturing regulations. Fire and safety systems should be functioning well. You will need several types of insurance: general liability, property, workers' comp, disability, a federal whiskey bond, and car insurance on your delivery vehicle. If you have a tasting room, you may want specific insurance, called dram-shop liability, that relates to establishments that serve alcohol.

Then you must decide on equipment. Inevitably, you will need a mashing vessel, fermenters, and a still. All of this can be done very low tech or with specialized equipment. We have fermented in plastic 50-gallon drums—a very inexpensive solution, but without temperature control afforded by professional fermenters. Prosumer stills can be purchased for just over $1,000, but capacity will be limited. Professional craft-sized stills, manufactured by Forsyths, Vendome, Christian Carl, or Kothe, run anywhere from $40,000 to $100,000. Plumbing and electrifying the space may be a substantial cost. If you are distilling from grain, a forklift and a grain mill will likely come in handy. As will a bottling machine, since the turkey baster and funnel method gets very tedious.

You will need packaging and labels, which must be designed, approved, registered, and printed. Wax and corks or caps will need to be sourced. Boxes and packing material will be necessary, as will a delivery vehicle, if you are self-distributing. For our first year, I assumed we would make deliveries in a backpack via subway, but this was woefully naive. You will need a car (ours is a generously donated 1991 Geo Metro named Lisa) and gas.

After that you still need to be sure someone wants to buy your product, and so you will spend time courting liquor stores and bars in your own state and distributors in other states. You will need posters, perhaps, and you will be very tempted to include all those brilliant taglines you keep thinking of. You will need to spend time behind a table pouring tastes of your product, entertaining people who want to talk your ear off about how wrongly you are doing everything as

The chalkboards helped us manage two shifts a day, seven days a week, tracking various batches as they worked through the mashing, fermenting, stripping, and spiriting steps of the process.

they ask for seconds on their quarter-ounce taste of whiskey. They will also boggle your mind with the myths and misrepresentations that they repeat to you about whiskey, and maybe you will feel like correcting them, or maybe not, because, after all, the customer is always right.

And you will lose money—quite a lot of it. But just maybe, at a certain point, you will be right in thinking that you can quit your day job. There may be hurricanes and floods and fires and broken bottles and infestations of mice, but maybe one day you will decide that it was worth it.

FLOOR PLAN OF A CRAFT DISTILLERY

This suggests the layout of a 3,500-square-foot (325 sq m) craft distillery, capable of distilling 500 gallons (1,892 L) of mash in a day in two runs, making about 35–40 gallons (132–150 L) of distillate from each run, or a little more than a 53-gallon (200-L) barrel each day. This drawing shows a 250-gallon (946-L) wash still, a 165-gallon (625-L) spirit still, five open-top oak fermenters, and a 250-gallon (946-L) mash cooker. While certainly not necessary, there is also a shop and tasting room, as many small distilleries

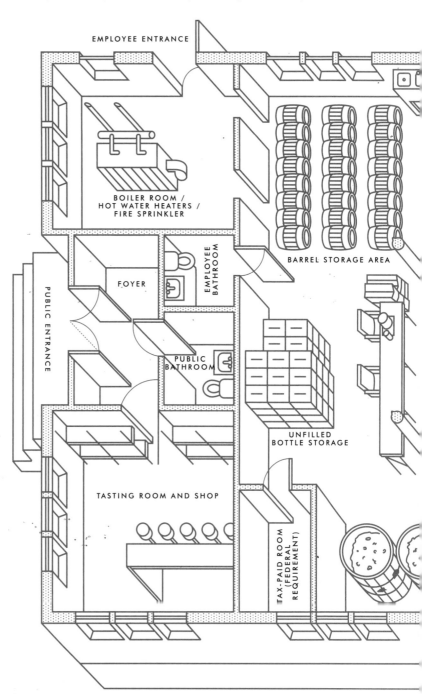

EMPLOYEE ENTRANCE

BOILER ROOM /
HOT WATER HEATERS /
FIRE SPRINKLER

BARREL STORAGE AREA

FOYER

EMPLOYEE
BATHROOM

PUBLIC ENTRANCE

PUBLIC
BATHROOM

UNFILLED
BOTTLE STORAGE

TASTING ROOM AND SHOP

TAX-PAID ROOM
(FEDERAL
REQUIREMENT)

benefit from offering tours and selling direct to customers. There is a small area devoted to barrel aging, though what is shown is much smaller than what would be needed to run at capacity. Many small distillers store barrels offsite in a bonded warehouse.

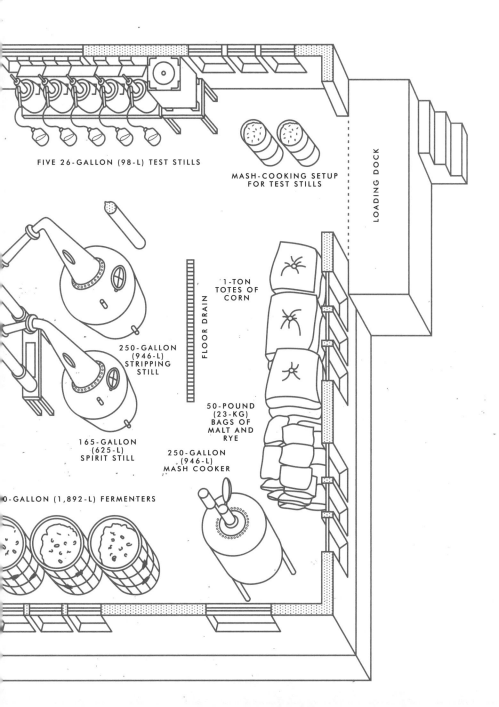

FIVE 26-GALLON (98-L) TEST STILLS

MASH-COOKING SETUP
FOR TEST STILLS

LOADING DOCK

1-TON
TOTES OF
CORN

FLOOR DRAIN

250-GALLON
(946-L)
STRIPPING
STILL

50-POUND
(23-KG)
BAGS OF
MALT AND
RYE

165-GALLON
(625-L)
SPIRIT STILL

250-GALLON
(946-L)
MASH COOKER

0-GALLON (1,892-L) FERMENTERS

"I'll pour you the first one and after that,
     if you don't have one, it's your own fucking
     fault. You know where it is."

—KINGSLEY AMIS

CHAPTER FIVE

HOW TO DRINK WHISKEY

I'm not really going to tell you how to drink whiskey. I don't know that one way is necessarily any better than all the others, and as long as you are drinking whiskey, I would say the battle is won. But there are still decisions to be made, and they are worth being thoughtful about.

The Home Bar

For most of my twenties, I never bothered to keep much alcohol around my apartment. But as my position on entertaining shifted away from cramming people into the apartment to pound cheap beers, a home bar began to feel like a very hospitable thing to develop: a few bottles of carefully chosen whiskey to offer friends who drop by. And while I was raised to view a home bar as something bourgeois and suburban, I now view it as an opportunity to be something of an instigator.

It has taken a long time to put together my home bar, and the collection is not nearly as considered as I'd like. Also, since I happen to be a hoarder when it comes to whiskey, most of the bottles are unopened. This is wrong. Whiskey should be drunk and not saved. The distillers do the saving for you; that is the whole point of having millions of barrels of whiskey in warehouses and not, for example, your living room.

So I have come to accept that my own bar is flawed, and have begun to imagine a perfect one instead. It would have around a dozen bottles, which affords concision without being too constraining. There would need to be one bottle of non-whiskey, for the guests who aren't yet enlightened, as well as vermouth, liqueurs, and bitters for mixing.

But what should those dozen-or-so bottles be? I posed this question to a couple of whiskey-drinking friends: Jonathan Wingo, former shopkeeper at the Whiskey Shop in Brooklyn, who worked as a tour guide at Kings County and is now brand ambassador for the Balvenie; and Allison Patel, a blogger as the Whiskey Woman and brand owner of Brenne, a French single malt whiskey. The challenge was articulated: a selection of bottles (not necessarily considering price) that reflects the breadth of whiskeys available, both domestic and from distilleries abroad. Here are each of our ideal home bars.

Colin's home bar focuses mostly on American whiskeys.

COLIN'S BAR

Start with a classic, rye-recipe Kentucky bourbon. In this category, I'm partial to **Woodford Reserve** for a lot of reasons—though I concede taste is only one of them—and it is, in my mind, the archetypal bourbon. You might also include a wheated bourbon like Maker's Mark, or Larceny from Heaven Hill, but my pick is **W. L. Weller**. I like to have a bottle of something really old, mostly for the novelty of it; I have an unopened bottle of **Elijah Craig 21** that was distilled at Heaven Hill before the fire and around the time I got out of class for the summer after my sixth grade. Since I'm probably never going to drink that one, I'm going to have to save up for another bottle, and you really don't have to spend a lot of money to get an excellent bourbon. Wild Turkey is probably the best value in whiskey today—it's as good as you can get for the price— but my pick for my home bar is **Old Grand-Dad**, which is a sentimental favorite. I really like the bottle, which can be used to guide airplanes to their gates in case you find yourself on the tarmac without the usual orange baton.

For rye, **Bulleit Rye** is a good value among all the many LDI ryes and probably will look nicest on your shelf. For craft ryes, the options are a little slim, but I think Hudson's **Manhattan Rye** is nice—heavy on the wood, but with an independent, authentic character.

I'm not sure it deserves its own discussion independent of bourbon, but for Tennessee whiskey, there aren't a lot of options right now. There are variants of George Dickel and variants of Jack Daniel's. Craft Tennessee whiskeys include Collier and McKeel and Prichard's, though Prichard's does not use the Lincoln County Process, and state law now mandates it for all other distillers intent on making Tennessee whiskey. My pick is **Dickel No. 12**.

Corn whiskey is too often ignored as a category, even though it was once a very common spirit, especially in the South, and it is the only unaged whiskey written into law. It can be aged or unaged, and while I prefer completely unaged, I also like two options that are on the market: **Mellow Corn**, which comes in a cool retro bottle and is cheap enough that you could buy a lifetime supply up front, and **True Blue** from Balcones, which is nutty and spicy, made from blue corn.

For white whiskey, Death's Door and Jacob's Ghost are options that are easier to find, whereas I have not been able to find the unaged whiskeys from House Spirits that are often mentioned with reverence. Craft distillers generally do better than commercial distillers in this category, since age is removed as a variable. Right now I like Koval's wheat whiskey, but **Low Gap** is my pick for this bar.

Among craft spirits, the field is still pretty wide open, but often the nontraditional categories of American whiskeys (like wheat and malt whiskeys) have interesting entrants. I add New Holland's **Brewers' Whiskey**; they do an excellent malt whiskey, and this one is classic. For wheat whiskey, Breuckelen's **77 Whiskey** (the wheat variety) is very true to the base grain.

I also include a bottle of **Kings County Moonshine**, both because I like it and because if you do make your own whiskey, you should obviously have it in your collection.

Even American whiskey zealots should have a bottle or two of scotch around as an olive branch for foreign or unenlightened visitors.

For a blended scotch, I like Johnnie Walker Green Label pretty well—
it's a blend of malt whiskeys and is a little more flavorful—but I think
the **Famous Grouse** is a great bottle for any collection, purely based
on branding. Among single malts, a heavily peated Islay malt like
Laphroaig is good for extending what you can offer to a guest.

To round out your bar, you'll need a bottle of something
that isn't whiskey. A London gin is probably an innocuous add to the
collection, and most London gins have nice packaging. American craft
gins can be quite creative and unusual, though they can get so creative
that you wonder if what you are drinking really belongs in the gin
category.

Finally you'll want a bottle of bitters and a bottle of vermouth,
both of which are often used in whiskey cocktails. Angostura bitters
are the old standby, but bitters too are experiencing a renaissance of
interest, and a variety of new flavors are being offered, sometimes as
a gift set, which is a good way to add a lot of choices to your bar.
Sweet vermouth is an ingredient in the Manhattan, while dry vermouth
is typically used in making martinis but also works well with white
whiskeys. **Dolin's Dry Vermouth** makes a nice white Manhattan, with
white whiskey in place of the bourbon.

Jonathan's home bar is a mixture of small-label Kentucky whiskeys, craft spirits, and some international entries.

JONATHAN'S BAR

My ideal whiskey bar reflects what I enjoy most about whiskey: the diversity in tastes. Admittedly, in our booming micro- and craft-distilling times, sometimes a distillery fails to ask the question, "Just because I can, does that mean I should?" So, these are the whiskeys that I want around not only to celebrate great differences in flavor and innovation, but also because they are delicious.

I try to keep a balance of whiskeys that either facilitate conversation or become conversation. Let's start with bourbon to greet guests. **Corner Creek** is a sourced bourbon put out by a couple of well-meaning dudes from Miami way back at the start of the sourced-whiskey scene. Kentucky Bourbon Distillers bottles this for them, so I'm not sure of the provenance, but I really do love the vague mash bill. This super-soft whiskey flexes four grains and a fun finish. This and **Johnny Drum Private Stock**, another from Kentucky Bourbon Distillers, are my backyard, Solo-cup bourbons when the party is existing outside of the glass. For my mid-range bourbon, I love the final blending done on the sourced whiskey in **Breaking & Entering** from St. George Spirits. They highlight a slightly different face of bourbon that is particularly tasty. On the top-shelf side of things, I order **William Larue Weller** from the Sazerac Antique Collection anytime I see it on a back bar because it proves difficult to stock at home. I love that mature, wheated-bourbon smell! A couple of drops of water in this, and you'll look like an idiot for the next twenty minutes keeping the glass under your nose.

In terms of rye, I like what Finger Lakes Distilling is doing with their **McKenzie Rye** by finishing (or oxidizing) in used New York sherry-esque wine barrels. I always keep a bottle of **Willett Family Estate Rye** (I like the 4 year), because I think LDI rye is awesome at 110 proof. Speaking of LDI rye, Smooth Ambler was able to showcase maturity with their **Old Scout 7 Year Rye**. Seek out Anchor's **Old Potrero 18th Century Style** bottles from the old proof around 127. It packs all the rye spice with a new oak funk. Corsair's **Ryemageddon** rules and, with its malty chocolatey roast, gives rye a finish. It never hurts to keep a bottle of **Old Overholt** around for the fun party trick of infusing it for two days with raisins or caraway seeds or cloves. It's a winner every time.

Single malts shuffle in and out for me. I have a few staples. **St. George Single Malt** is a whiskey that everyone I meet must try. Their distillate is superb and the maturation is unique. The bouquet is incredible and the flavor is familiar. The **Balvenie 14 Year Caribbean Cask** features the already awesome Balvenie, which is then finished in a barrel used to age rum. Fair warning: You may find it hard to keep this bottle full. The Suntory **Hakushu 12 Year** is a peated Japanese whiskey with a crisp fruit finish, so the delicate smoke doesn't loiter on your tongue. For a more oily, bacon smoke, I enjoy the peated Tobermory whiskey called **Ledaig 10 Year** from the Isle of Mull. On the luxurious end of things, the **Balvenie 21 Year Port Wood** is a masterpiece whiskey that if you share, proves you're generous—and if you don't, proves you're sane. The Balcones **#1 Single Malt Texas Whiskey** is an un-shy, rich whiskey that gives salute to other malt whiskey with an ornery Texas grin.

Now for the specialty products. Nothing feels quite as good to drink on a rooftop staring down at the city than **Kings County Moonshine**. Super earthy, and embracing that Brooklyn funk with some subtle sweet notes of the grain, it gets the job done and is shareable! Colin might find it easy to dismiss the hopped whiskeys, but I cannot. That stuff is great . . . when done well. **Charbay Whiskey #2** is a showpiece on any bar with its price point, but holy goalie, does it taste great. You can grab more approachable versions in the aged R5 or the Double and Twisted. Long Island Spirits is making **Pine Barrens Single Malt** from distilled beer from Blue Point Brewery. It tastes like concentrated beer, with a malty beery finish. From Ireland, you should pick up a jug of **Locke's 8 Year**. It's a close-to-mothballed project from the Cooley Distillery that you can still see on the Celtic Whiskey Shop website. If you are ever in the mood for a barbecue in your mouth in liquid form, keep a bottle of **Brimstone** from Balcones at the bar. Those smoky oils will be with you for your next meal.

You should also have your preferred trio for a negroni, green Chartreuse VEP, bubbles, and a bottle of Hermitage for all of those places that whiskey can't take you.

I already hate this list. It's pedantic, new and yet outdated, not easy to find, and gaping with holes. I already have regrets over missed gems. But that's what is great about our time—we can always try something new or different. And I assure you the juice in this list is good.

Allison's bar focuses more on European and scotch-style whiskies, with a few craft entries and cocktail spirits.

ALLISON'S BAR

I used to think having a bottle or two of whiskey open at a time was plenty. But as my curiosity grew, so did my appreciation for a variety of styles from distilleries all around the world. Now my personal collection includes more than two hundred open bottles of whiskey and I'd say it still has a lot of holes.

However, should you approach rounding out your own collection with a bit more clarity from the beginning, then my suggestion would be to have a healthy selection of drams from what I call "whiskeys from nontraditional countries"—that is, from places other than Scotland, Ireland, the United States, and Canada. It's not that these places aren't making wonderful spirits, but it can be fruitful to embrace the concept of "terroir" and push your whiskey exploration to new locales. It's how I came to produce my own single malt, Brenne, from the Cognac region of France. Atypical? Yes. But also refreshingly different.

As for your own whiskey bar, my recommendations—at the moment—would be categorized by whiskeys for sipping and those for cocktails. (Not that they aren't interchangeable!)

SIPPING

This is my favorite way to enjoy a good whiskey. It's clean and simple and allows for the complexity of the spirit to properly reveal itself. Don't be afraid to add a few drops of water to your dram, which will allow it to really open up. In no particular order: **Mackmyra** is a refreshing single malt from Sweden that is difficult but not impossible to find in the United States. (Only one expression is available at the moment.) The **Balvenie Double Wood 12 Year** is a non-peated Scottish single malt that is easy drinking year round. Suntory **Yamazaki 12 Year**, a Japanese single malt, works well neat or on the rocks. If you have deep pockets, spend up for the 18 year; it's extremely rich and complex. **Compass Box Peat Monster** is a unique peated Scotch whisky that is a careful blend of single malts from Islay and Speyside. This is a lovely, smoky dram for curling up with around a fire. **Brenne Estate Cask**, an elegant single malt whiskey from France, is an unexpected crowd pleaser, very smooth and approachable. It's great for your novices and experts alike. Try **Kavalan Soloist** for an excellent cask-strength sherry-bomb from another unusual place: Taiwan. Though keep in mind that this will need to be purchased abroad as it's not (yet) available Stateside. **Koval Dark Millet** is a conscious choice for your gluten-free guests. **Pappy Van Winkle**: It's anyone's guess where you can find this American cult favorite's annual allocations, but if you ever see a bottle for sale, snatch it up. And Balcones **Rumble** is the non-whiskey that drinks like a whiskey and will turn your skeptical friends into whiskey drinkers, too.

COCKTAILS

Many people now make Manhattans regularly at home. I prefer making them with rye instead of bourbon, which in addition to being more classically correct offers a more balanced cocktail. The spice of the rye whiskey is a better-suited partner for your vermouth choice (sweet vermouth for a regular Manhattan, a 50/50 split of sweet and dry vermouth for a Perfect Manhattan). **Old Overholt** is my choice for an easy, affordable rye. I suggest **Gentleman Jack Tennessee Whiskey** if you want to give your guests a bourbon option; it'll do just fine. And as for white whiskeys, try Corsair **Wry Moon.** White whiskeys are here to stay, and I enjoy having them around to make a more interesting Bloody Mary, or to sip on with citrus-based desserts.

And finally, a tip for the aesthetically conscious: It is a sad truth that some great whiskeys are sold in cheesy bottles. If you don't like how the bottle looks next to your other whiskeys, pour it into a decanter. This will immediately elevate the overall look of your bar.

Cocktails and Other Extensions
of Whiskey Appreciation

For the last twenty years, any spirit that isn't scotch has been viewed primarily not as a sipping spirit but as an ingredient for cocktails. This is regrettable. To me, the pleasure of whiskey is in the nuance of its flavor and the intensity of the spirit. But of course I'm biased—if you spend as much time laboring over the spirit as we do, you hesitate to sully it with Canada Dry. I'm not quite sure how the Scots have managed to ensure that their whiskey never ends up in cocktails, or only very rarely. Maybe it's because of the taste of their product or the price of their bottles, or maybe it's just respect for their long, careful process. I once, in more naive days, tried to order a Famous Grouse and Coke, I guess confusing it for a more upscale version of Wild Turkey. I was looked at with pity and disdain, though I'm not sure if it was because the bartender thought it was the pollution of such a beverage or simply a sense that the resultant taste would not meet approval. I was given a Jack and Coke instead.

That said, not everyone wants to drink 100-proof liquor straight, or even over ice. I'm sympathetic to that, and that is certainly where the cocktail comes in, especially for formal settings. The problem with cocktail culture in cities like New York is that it has become an arms race. You can wait in line for an hour to be admitted to a bar where they charge a small fortune for a hibiscus-infused, whipped-egg-white amaretto mescal with bourbon, served with a hand-carved ice cube and a twist of licorice root imported from Tobago. The one-upmanship, driven by an attempt to make each sip distinctive, often has the opposite effect, flattening the experience of drinking a cocktail and making us all feel like extras in each other's period films. What's lost is a sense of humor and personality, which comes directly from the person making the drink.

Not everyone has the time or inclination to make whiskey, but we can all make a drink. Making a drink is political, at once diplomatic and socially charged. It can be an act of flirtation or commiseration, but it is always an invitation to escalate the act of spending time together. Cocktails often appear at life's articulation points: celebrations, commencements, turns of fortune. They dress up an occasion.

Perhaps the best way to think about cocktails is as inventive solutions to the problem of what to do with whiskey. Home distillers face this problem acutely. Yes, you will want to treat your precious spirit carefully. But after having produced a handful of runs, you may get antsy, and wonder whether some of your product is missing one final step. You may be curious about how bitters interact with corn whiskey—and then start to think about making bitters yourself. You may find the urge to cook with your bourbon, or the barrel it was aged in.

Over the following pages, we invited friends of the distillery—neighbors, loyal customers, current and former employees—to recommend things to do with the whiskey we've made. We also asked them to tell a story about whiskey, the distillery, or something personal about their recipe—whatever makes the recipe more than just something imbibable or comestible. Whiskey and storytelling go nicely together, so perhaps this will jump-start your own thinking. I'll start.

MINT JULEP

BY COLIN SPOELMAN

One weekend when I was in college, I was tasked with making mint juleps. It was the day of the Kentucky Derby my junior year, which fell during final exams, but this was my right and responsibility as a Kentuckian, and so I offered. Trouble was, I'm an *Appalachian* Kentuckian, which is a very different thing from a *Bluegrass* Kentuckian. Such distinctions were subtleties that no one cared about up North, even if they defined my youth. (If my college friends only knew the childhood anxiety and excitement that came from visiting the sophisticated metropolis of Lexington!) Regardless, I had no idea how to make a julep, but to admit that ignorance was to forfeit any credibility I had as a Southerner, which was the broad justification I used to explain my eccentricities and ignorances in most cultural matters.

Fortunately this was the dawn of the Internet age, and I found a recipe online. A few recipes, actually. Recalling that ice is important to the julep, I selected the one that called for a blender. Or maybe I only intuited that a blender would be necessary. As it turns out, you cannot liquefy mint in a blender, nor is that required or desired in a julep. But I thought it would be great.

Into the blender went the bourbon, the ice, and a bundle of mint sprigs, as well as a lot of powdered sugar. The result was a bourbon mint smoothie, flecked with vegetal bits that gave it the consistency of a chopped salad. It was very, very wrong, and I was told so. Undeterred, I removed myself from the party we had planned and drank mine in private, which helped quite a bit.

Mint juleps are properly made with sugar syrup; often this is infused overnight with mint. I would recommend skipping all this. Throughout most of American history, drinks were made using a lot of sugar—it seems that old recipes were designed for palates that weren't already inundated with high-fructose corn syrup. Also, if you use rye in your julep, it becomes a *Yankee cooler* and is no longer a mint julep. You are trying too hard.

RECIPE:
silver cup
4 sprigs mint
2½ ounces (74 ml) bourbon
crushed ice
seltzer

Frost a silver cup in your freezer. Remove the stems from
3 mint sprigs and place the leaves in the bottom of a silver
cup. Add a splash of bourbon and muddle the mint. Add the
rest of the bourbon, pack the cup with crushed ice, and then
fill with seltzer. Garnish with the remaining mint sprig.

OLD FASHIONED

BY DAVID HASKELL

A few weeks after Colin and I brought our bootleg whiskey operation above ground, I toured my family around the new distillery. We had graduated from Colin's kitchen, and secured a license, but our set-up was barely larger than what you might have seen in a bootlegger's bathroom: one small room, five hobby stills, and a bunch of tubs of fermenting mash. It looked and smelled bizarre to everyone except my grandfather, James Grant, who said it reminded him of his father, Havens.

Havens had grown up in Jamestown, a small town in western New York near where much of the state's grain is grown, and where Kings County's corn is sourced. After college and law school, Havens took a job in New York City, and in 1922 married Carolyn Hall, a poet who wore to her wedding a navy blue gown and a lavender hat. They settled a few miles north of the city and started a family. Havens was a shy, nervous man with few friends. (He was described in a college alumni report as "the man who dwelt among us without interest or inquiry as to the progress or affairs of his fellows.") But it seems he lived a rich hobbyist's life. In elementary school he founded a small newspaper, the *Jamestown Post,* and as a young adult he volunteered at an early radio station. He gardened, collected stamps and coins, and developed photographs in his darkroom. He was, in his son's words, an "inveterate independent creator." Which is likely what led him to run a small whiskey distillery out of his basement in Scarsdale.

My grandfather remembers his father returning from work in the city, and then spending his evenings downstairs, where the air smelled of corn mash. He doesn't think Havens ever sold his whiskey, or recall any social events at which it was served. It was just another of his father's projects. "I suspect he just loved to produce the bottles," he told me.

When Havens did drink, it was often an Old Fashioned, which had been invented at the Pendennis Club in Louisville and introduced to New York via the Waldorf Astoria Hotel bar. There are dozens of variations, using different base whiskeys, different bitters, and different citrus. In the 1930s, when Havens was distilling, someone introduced oranges and maraschino cherries to the mix. I vote yes to the orange, no to the cherry, and to keep the cocktail spicy and strong by starting with a high-proof rye.

RECIPE:

½ teaspoon sugar

2 dashes Angostura bitters

2 dashes orange bitters

2 ounces (60 ml) high-proof rye

1 large ice cube

1 strip lemon peel

1 thin orange slice

Muddle the sugar and the bitters in a whiskey glass. Add the rye and ice, and stir well. Twist the lemon peel over the top and drop it in. Slip the orange slice onto the rim.

MANHATTAN

BY ST. JOHN FRIZELL, OWNER OF FORT DEFIANCE

I can't remember the first Manhattan I ever tasted, but I remember the man who taught me how to make them. My grandfather, Leon, was a chemist and pharmacist; he was kind, but he was also cautious and precise, which I was not. The order he imposed in his immaculate home, a split-level ranch in suburban New Jersey, terrified me as a child. I tried to stay out from under his feet during the afternoons I spent there after school, but it seemed I was always spilling milk on his tablecloth or tracking something onto his wall-to-wall carpet.

When he got his liquor bottles down from the high shelf, I tried especially hard not to disturb him. Once or twice a week, he would assemble on his Formica countertop the Canadian whisky, the sweet vermouth, and the fascinating little bottle of bitters with the oversize label, as well as a Pyrex beaker and stir rod. Leon measured his ingredients exactly, bending over to see where the edge of the meniscus landed, and stirred to combine them, before carefully pouring the resulting analgesic elixir into bottles with a stainless-steel funnel. These he would label "Manhattan" in a careful hand and store in the refrigerator. In those days, a cocktail hour did not pass without my grandparents enjoying a Manhattan on the rocks, complete with a maraschino cherry, at the kitchen table.

Years later, my mother told me that my grandfather's cocktails were legendary in the neighborhood when she was a child in the 1950s; that my grandparents' parties would spill out of the rec room, into the front yard, and onto the street. I wish I could have dropped by one of those parties, not just to taste the cocktails, which I'm sure were impeccable, but to watch Leon the party host behind his home bar, stirring cocktails and smiling complacently as his guests tracked all kinds of things onto his wall-to-wall carpet.

2 ounces (60 ml) Canadian blended whisky

1 ounce (30 ml) sweet vermouth

2 dashes Angostura bitters

maraschino cherry

Stir over ice and strain. Garnish with a maraschino cherry and serve straight up.

CHERRY BOUNCE

BY SARAH LOHMAN,
HISTORIAN AND AUTHOR OF FOURPOUNDSFLOUR.COM

I make my living as a historic gastronomist: I explore the history of food as a way to connect to the past and to inspire my contemporary cooking. Often my work starts with personal stories, ephemera, or an intriguing historic detail that conjures to mind a flavor I'd like to explore. For example, I recently learned of a recipe tucked inside Martha Washington's leather memorandum book titled "To Make Excellent Cherry Bounce."

Cherry Bounce is a cordial made by steeping cherries in alcohol; her recipe is made with brandy, but by the nineteenth century—when the first printed versions of Cherry Bounce appeared—whiskey was the alcohol of choice. According to the historians at Mount Vernon, the Washington recipe isn't in Martha's handwriting, so I like to think of her partying at some government shindig, sipping on red liqueur, and asking for the recipe. It inspired me to try my own hand at Cherry Bounce.

RECIPE:
2 cups (310 g) fresh cherries, a blend of sour Morello
    and sweet, pitted
4 cups (946 ml) whiskey
1 teaspoon almond extract
¼ cup (50 g) sugar

Historically, there's a lot of variation in how this recipe can be made, which leaves plenty of room for modern interpretation. The simplest method is to add the cherries to a large mason jar, and cover them with whiskey and sugar. Shake the jar every day for a week and you'll have a delicate cherry-flavored potation. You can leave it as is and pour a bit when you want it, or you can strain the cherries and save them for a treat. Or mash them, strain them again, and add the juice back to the whiskey.

Many recipes called for additional flavorings: Martha Washington's suggested cinnamon, cloves, and nutmeg; others included ginger and mace. Some recipes recommended cracking the cherry pits and adding them to the infusion; small amounts of arsenic in the pits add an almond flavor. I suggest adding almond extract instead.

Traditional Cherry Bounce is left to infuse for at least a month, but it can be left for up to six, which means that by New Year's Day, George and Martha could have opened a well-aged bottle to share with guests.

TODDIES, HOT AND COLD

BY ROBERT MOOR, FORMER DISTILLER

When I first started working at Kings County in the summer of 2010, I was delighted to find that the job provided ample time to read. Each batch of whiskey began in a flurry, as one juggled a series of tasks like a line cook, but ended in a hush, with little to do but watch the languorous drip of the stills. Perhaps it was the environment, but as I burned through book after book, I became keenly aware of how an author's drink of choice could perfume the pages of a novel. Fitzgerald's very language is redolent of the gin rickey. Kerouac stinks of tequila, Chandler of gimlets, Hemingway of mojitos and red wine. Wilde fumes with absinthe and Poe with cognac, while Burroughs somehow manages to isolate the weird chemical frequencies in a vodka and Coke. Anne Sexton drank straight vodka, whereas Sylvia Plath wrote about vodka but mostly drank wine. Carson McCullers was cold-blooded, so she drank sherry mixed with hot tea in the morning and straight bourbon at night. Bourbon was also the poison of Sherwood Anderson, Dylan Thomas, Walker Percy, and Ring Lardner. Steinbeck preferred brandy, but when he couldn't get it during Prohibition, he appeared at a Stanford-Berkeley football game wearing an overcoat lined with vials of grain alcohol, pilfered from a chemistry lab where he worked.

And then there is Faulkner, the poet laureate of corn whiskey. I read *Light in August* over the course of about seven shifts that summer. A significant portion of the book concerns the exploits of a pair of bootleggers—a topic with which Faulkner was familiar, having run boatfuls of illegal whiskey into New Orleans during Prohibition. There are lovely passages describing the act of drinking whiskey, which goes down "cold as molasses" before beginning its slow, warm uncoiling. Hemingway once wrote that in Faulkner he could detect the "boozy courage of corn whiskey." (He meant it as an insult, but Faulkner likely wouldn't have taken it as such.) Sherwood Anderson recalls that when he first met Faulkner in New Orleans, in 1925, Faulkner showed up wearing an overcoat that "bulged strangely, so much, that at first glance, I thought he must be in some queer way deformed." Faulkner informed Anderson that he intended to stay for some time in the city, and asked if he could leave some things at Anderson's house. "His 'things' consisted of some six or eight half gallon jars of moon liquor he had brought with him from the country that were stowed in the pockets of the big coat." For breakfast, Faulkner would eat beignets with a glass of corn liquor, and as he wrote, he kept a jug or three under his desk.

Faulkner's favorite drink is often listed as the mint julep, which is probably right: His house in Oxford still displays his beloved metal julep cup. But his old standby was the simpler and subtler toddy, which he writes of "compounding . . . with ritualistic care." It comes in two forms, hot and cold. Faulkner's niece, Dean Faulkner Wells, recalls her uncle making hot toddies and serving them to his ailing children on a silver tray. But unlike today, the cold toddy seems to have been the more popular in Faulkner's day.

RECIPE:

1 teaspoon (4 g) sugar

4 ounces (120 ml) water (cold or boiling)

2 ounces (60 ml) bourbon or white whiskey

if cold, 1 lemon slice; if hot, ½ lemon; for both, juice
and rind

The key to a toddy, according to Faulkner, is that the sugar must be dissolved into a small amount of water before the whiskey is added; otherwise it "lies in a little intact swirl like sand at the bottom of the glass." (One of Faulkner's short stories, "An Error in Chemistry," hinges on this point: A Northern murderer, pretending to be a Southern gentleman, mistakenly mixes sugar with "raw whiskey"; the Southerners recognize his faux pas and immediately pounce on him.) Once the sugar is dissolved, the whiskey is poured over it. Top it off, to taste, with the remaining water—preferably, Faulkner writes, "rainwater from a cistern." Add lemon and serve in a heavy glass tumbler.

GARDEN COCKTAIL

BY BRIANNA HALSTEAD, TASTING-ROOM MANAGER

When I first began drinking whiskey, it was usually lifted from an older sibling—mine or a friend's. I am sure that this helped it taste better, because we were probably drinking whatever bottom-shelf swill these teenage siblings could barter outside of a Circle K. I grew up in Las Vegas, and as I think back about drinking there, I think shot-and-a-beer kind of nights. I never sipped whiskey, or had a real cocktail.

I grew up and landed in Los Angeles. I was nineteen. I began working for an influential chef and restaurant group that was known for being involved in the farm-to-table movement. The owners took me under their wing—I went from answering the phones and taking reservations to handling finances and haggling deals. The bar program there had no rules, and the bartenders opted to go to the farmers' markets on their time off to come up with fresh cocktails using local produce. It was with them that I had my first Manhattan and Old Fashioned, and then tried variations of cocktails made with avocado or Buddha's hand citron. No one in Hollywood was doing this at the time, and it felt like we were on the forefront of something.

Six years later, I moved to New York and became involved in Kings County by way of nagging Colin. I started to understand my palate better, and learned to sip whiskey. This garden cocktail is inspired by my roots in the food business, and those farmers'-market-obsessed bartenders who taught me that you can be creative with cocktails. I find the sweetness of the corn in Kings County Distillery Moonshine pairs well with tart tomato and lime. I'm writing this in June and foresee drinking many more of these during this summer's BBQ season.

RECIPE:

8 leaves fresh cilantro (or to taste)

4 halved cherry or grape tomatoes

1 ounce (30 ml) simple syrup

1 ounce (30 ml) freshly squeezed lime juice

2 ounces (60 ml) Kings County Moonshine

ice

seltzer (optional)

Muddle the cilantro and tomatoes. Add all other ingredients. Shake vigorously. Pour in a 6- to 8-ounce glass and enjoy. If feeling adventurous, serve in a tall glass and top with seltzer.

RUMBLE SEAT

BY TRISTAN WILLEY, FORMER DISTILLER

I worked at the distillery for only a year and a half, but I was twenty-three and new to New York, and the distillery is what made me. It's where I found my connection to booze, made and lost friends, ended a long relationship, started the rest of my life, and established my foothold in the city. Toiling alone in a 107-degree room over boiling mash and dripping stills can amplify some thoughts, and numb others. I could never tell if it granted me complete understanding of how to tackle the world, or just let me hide from it for eight hours at a time. But making whiskey was the happiest and most satisfied I have ever been.

After spending so much time alone with raw ingredients, you begin to bond with the process. I swear I knew everything about each batch I made—the slight variation in the ingredients, the funkiness of the yeast, the music that had been playing, the mood I was in, the weather outside. One summer day at the distillery, after having just hauled in a metric ton of barley, I was catching my breath when the room began to wobble. The raw corn distillate in a large glass carboy, which I had been using as a footrest, began to slosh side to side, then thump against the lid and threaten to spill. I looked around the room full of shaking liquid and thought: *This is it. This is the day our poorly constructed second-floor loft simply buckles under the weight of a distillery. Our ship is going down.* Only after noticing the traffic light outside slap like a metronome did I come to terms with my first earthquake. I paced the room, calmed myself with a swig of product, and marked the day's batches with an X. I swear you could taste the difference.

Later that year, I left the distillery to work in cocktails, first at Amor y Amargo and later at Booker & Dax. Together with my friend Chris Elford, who also distilled at Kings County, I spent a long time creating a corn whiskey cocktail. Moonshine is not always the malleable ingredient you want it to be—it doesn't always play nice. But we finally bullied it into a recipe that feels worthy of our time as distillers. We call it a Rumble Seat.

RECIPE:

1½ ounces (45 ml) Kings County Moonshine

½ ounce (15 ml) Lillet White

¼ ounce (7 ml) Cocchi Americano

6 dashes Luxardo Maraschino

8 drops Bittermens Mole Bitters

Stir and serve up in a coupe with no garnish.

NASCAR FIZZ

BY CHRIS ELFORD, FORMER DISTILLER

In my early twenties, I moved to Richmond, Virginia, mostly against my will. I had been coasting in my hometown, working odd jobs and living paycheck to paycheck. Eventually I got into some trouble with the wrong people and had to move a few hours away while things died down. I took a job at a BBQ restaurant, where I fell in love with beer, booze, and the comfort food of the South. Warm nights riding bikes and drinking Kentucky Gentleman (The Kage, I called it) in the former capital of the Confederacy sucked me in, and I became an honorary Southerner despite my Canadian roots. I read a lot of Mark Twain, took up smoking a pipe, and dreamed about going down the James River on a raft. I bought an old motorcycle.

Eventually I grew up, moved to New York City, and got serious about studying cocktails and beer. The New York thing kind of took too, strangely, and I found myself working as many jobs as I could to learn as much about booze as possible. In my last months in New York, I got an invite to Camp Runamok, a bourbon camp for bartenders held in Kentucky. I met my lady there, falling in love with her as we took turns taking pulls of a bottle of Larceny next to the campfire. I think the Southern air just makes me susceptible to these things.

A lot of what I like to do with whiskey is redeem maligned spirits as cocktail ingredients. Cocktails are not always about perfection, or finickiness. They can also be casual and resourceful—smart ways of dressing up low-quality liquor. So this recipe for a NASCAR Fizz calls for Virginia Lightning, but if you can't find that, then look for something that's oilier and not as clean as most boutique white dogs. Use the rough stuff. Or early experiments of your own.

RECIPE:

1 ounce (30 ml) Mellow Corn

1 ounce (30 ml) Virginia Lightning

½ ounce (15 ml) sorghum syrup (blended 1:1
with water)

½ ounce (15 ml) fresh lemon juice

½ ounce (15 ml) fresh lime juice

½ ounce (15 ml) almond milk

1 hefty dash Bittermens Elemakule Tiki Bitters

1 hefty dash Old Men Papaya Bitters

1 egg white

ice cubes

about 1 ounce (30 ml) malt liquor

In a shaker tin, vigorously shake all the ingredients
except the ice cubes and the malt liquor for 20 seconds.

Add the ice cubes and shake until ice cold.

Strain into a chilled Collins glass and top with the
malt liquor. I use Hurricane, but I don't pretend that
particular brand makes the drink.

NEW ORLEANS
SNO-BALL JULEP

BY HELEN HOLLYMAN, FORMER TASTING-ROOM MANAGER

I'm a part-time New Orleanian geographically speaking, and a full-time New Orleanian at heart. This city is beyond spectacular year round, but the heat during the dog days of summer is a force to be reckoned with. My antidote to reaching Blanche Dubois–status despair when the air conditioning gives out is to indulge in a sno-ball. (It's the same idea as a sno-cone, but you will hear a pin drop if you refer to it as such around these parts.) My other trick for the ultimate cooldown is a mint julep, so why not combine the two?

RECIPE:

½ cup (120 ml) whiskey

2 cups (400 g) sugar

½ cup (120 ml) freshly squeezed lemon juice, strained

¼ cup (10 g) fresh mint

crushed ice (enough to fill a glass)

condensed milk (optional)

In a saucepan over low heat, warm the whiskey with the sugar and lemon juice (make sure that it doesn't come to a boil). The goal is to make a boozy simple syrup.

Add the fresh mint and remove from the heat. Allow the mint to steep in the liquid while it cools to room temperature. Strain the mixture to remove the mint. This syrup will last up to a week in the refrigerator.

Fill a glass with crushed ice. Pack it down and shape the top with a form that looks like half of a sno-ball.

Give a generous New Orleans pour of the liquid on top of the crushed ice, or as much as you think you can handle without slurring your words. If you really want to go for it and have a proper sno-ball, pour some condensed milk on top and eat with a spoon.

PERFECT MANHATTAN

BY CHARLIE HORWICH, DISTILLER

I recently had to attend a wedding. Going through a heap of pants and shirts, corn stained and frayed from work, I decided to buy something new for the occasion. Clothing is not really my area of expertise, so for that reason, I'm glad there are formalities. I procured a suit, a tie, and a dress shirt, the holy trinity of men's formal wear. At which point I was ready to stand next to the bar and order a Perfect Manhattan.

The Manhattan is as formal a drink as it gets, neat but accented, and almost always appropriate. It is also quintessentially American, a true immigrant success story: Without the Italian sweet vermouth and the Trinidadian bitters, it would be just a glass of whiskey. (Even the maraschino cherry hails from Croatia, although purists leave it out.) Like anything American, its history is contested. I prefer the origin story that is certainly false—the one crediting the drink's invention to Jeanette Jerome, who, in 1874, is said to have hosted a fundraiser for gubernatorial candidate Samuel J. Tilden at the Manhattan Club in New York. At the time this event supposedly took place, Jerome was in Paris giving birth to Winston Churchill. But don't let the facts outweigh the poetry: The Brits got their Churchill just as we got our Manhattan, two champions of the modern world.

When I lean against a bar, I am liable to order anything. When I lean against a bar in a tie, it's with purpose, so I order a Manhattan. My Dad likes to say that his suit is his armor. I suppose a Manhattan is my shield; it gives me the courage to belong in a tie.

RECIPE:

2 ounces (60 ml) rye	2 dashes Angostura bitters
½ ounce (15 ml) sweet vermouth	maraschino cherry (optional)
½ ounce (15 ml) dry vermouth	

Stir over ice and strain. Try a maraschino cherry as garnish. Serve straight up.

PRESBYTERIAN

ANGELA SCHMITZ, BOTTLING MANAGER

My teenage self would hate me for saying this—I even have a hard time saying it now. The men in my family are my idols. They've been extremely influential, for better and for worse. My favorite childhood memories of growing up in Montana involve my older brothers Nick and Pete hunting porcupines, driving tractors, playing with firecrackers, and taking photographs; eventually sharing Marlboros, Old Milwaukee, and whiskey. Sometimes our Sunday church service was held at the amphitheater in Makoshika State Park, and afterward we'd explore the badlands, searching for dinosaur fossils and challenging each other to see who could climb to the top of the highest rocks. I would get scared, and they'd convince me to keep climbing.

I owe it to Nick for introducing me to the art of craft distilling, too. About a year ago, he asked me if I wanted to go on a tour of a distillery called Kings County. Sure, why not? We took the tour, and I fell in love, and when the tour guide asked if anyone wanted to volunteer on occasion, I put my name on the sign-up sheet. Little did they (or I) know that I would be showing up every weekend.

I sometimes wonder what I would be like without my male idols. Would I be some girly-girl interested in shopping for jewelry, high heels, and purses? Maybe drinking Cosmopolitans while tanning poolside? Who knows, but I'm enjoying my life for what it is, sometimes challenging and mostly simple. This recipe goes out to my family— thanks for introducing me to the simple life and constantly reminding me to "take it like a man."

RECIPE:

2 ounces (60 ml) bourbon

2 ounces (60 ml) ginger ale

2 ounces (60 ml) soda water

Pour bourbon over ice. Add ginger ale and soda water. Serve.

WHISKEY HIGHBALL

BY MARK BYRNE, FORMER DISTILLER

The most important words I ever heard on the subject of drinking were "Don't be so precious." It should stand to reason that I don't totally remember when exactly I heard them.

What I do know is that they came after a long period of misinformation. I spent most of my college years learning how to drink until I was sick, and the years immediately afterward teaching myself to fetishize everything on or above the middle shelf. I was taught to drink scotch with an eyedropper's worth of water, and the very precise instructions for making a Manhattan and an Old Fashioned. It took me a while to realize that this sort of obsession was just as much a chest-thumping ritual as the beer chugging I had suffered through in college, that carefully going through the motions was a way to avoid making a decision about what you wanted to drink, and that making a decision is the whole point. I started to ask myself, "What could I be doing that would make this more enjoyable? And why don't I just start doing that?"

These days, I drink whiskey in a simple highball cocktail. I water it down with seltzer, throw some superfine sugar in it, juice half a lemon. It tastes amazing. When my friends come over, I let them pick a bottle and then make it in huge batches. A bunch of lemons, a bunch of superfine, and if there are enough people, a half a bottle of really good whiskey. (I don't care about "wasting" fancy whiskey. Hell, I'll put Pappy in there.) For a little variation, you can do the whole thing with ginger ale, which makes it a proper Presbyterian . . . but then that's getting complicated again.

RECIPE:

2 parts whiskey

1 part fresh lemon juice

superfine sugar to taste, about a teaspoon

ice

seltzer to taste (usually equal to the amount of whiskey)

ABSINTHE

BY NATE LUCE, FORMER DISTILLER

A few months into working at Kings County, I became determined to make my own absinthe. I sought out St. John Frizell, my neighbor in Red Hook, Brooklyn, who owned the restaurant Fort Defiance, and was also a world-class bartender, a cocktail historian, and a former resident of New Orleans, where good absinthe is vital for the classic Sazerac. St. John told me that while great absinthe is most often made with a brandy base, before the recipe was codified in the late eighteenth century, there was a huge variety of local herbal remedies and digestifs made from whatever was on hand and of sufficiently high proof. It just so happened that, as a result of a slightly burned still at Kings County, I had access to a large quantity of Grade B+ unaged corn whiskey. And so I thought I would best honor tradition by using what I had on hand. Maybe the corn sweetness would come through, and the burnt smokiness would be buried by the herbal and bitter notes. . . .

I would say: Relative success? It was definitely pucker inducing at first, but eventually I was able to turn out something pretty delicious. There's certainly a bitter, woody undertone, and the strong anise presence means it won't be up your alley if you can't gobble black licorice. The deep, natural sweetness from the corn sugars makes it not too hard to drink, though, and gives a rounder drinking experience than mass-market absinthes that add refined sugar after the fact. Besides, bitterness is an undervalued flavor in the modern world. So much food and drink has been bleached of its naturally occurring bite that when I taste something like this it's a jolt to my senses, the Green Man grabbing me by my shoulders and shouting, "Are you seeing this?"

One September night, I snuck a couple bottles of my stuff home for a rooftop party in Red Hook, and everyone got tweaked out and schnockered. We looked west to Manhattan, where the spotlights of the 9/11 memorial were shimmering, blinking even. It was a magical, unsettling effect, which we later learned was caused by a flock of disoriented birds that had flown into the beams and become trapped in the blinding, fake daylight.

Among the reasons I love distilling are the spiritual, scientific, and historical through-lines of the craft. In one sense, it's the sole alchemical success story: There were recipes for finding the spirit of loaves of bread, the spirit of roosters, the spirit of gemstones, but only the spirit of beer and wine proved possible to divine. Absinthe adds another layer, with its herbalists and medicine men and doctors (some quacks) who used alcohol to find the spirits of various healthful herbs, and who retained some smidge of the pre-scientific traditional body of knowledge.

This experimental Kings County Absinthe is based on Dale Pendell's recipe from his essential *Pharmako/Poeia: Plant Powers, Poisons, and Herbcrafts*, though it uses less wormwood. Most ingredients can be found at a good, New Agey health-food store, or otherwise at MountainRoseHerbs.com. Note: Calamus (the root of a marsh grass sometimes called sweet flag) is not approved as a food additive by the FDA, and the amount of thujone, which comes from wormwood, is strictly limited in commercial absinthe. Both of these plants are alleged to be toxic to laboratory mice in high doses, but have been used and revered as medicine by traditional cultures. They're also both stimulants and visual clarifiers, and in my experience, they make the difference between a typical slow, sad drunkenness and an energetic, hyperaware intoxication. I suspect that the bans on these ingredients have more to do with fears of non-Western plant knowledge than actual health dangers, but regardless, Kings County—or you—would have to do without them if this was ever brought to market.

RECIPE:

22 grams wormwood

8.5 grams hyssop

1.8 grams calamus

30 grams anise seed

25 grams fennel seed

10 grams star anise

3.2 grams coriander seed

7.1 grams melissa

¾ gallon (2.8 L) distiller's strength (about 72 percent)
      homemade moonshine

4.2 grams mint

1 gram citron peel

4.2 grams licorice root

a little bit of lavender and ginger

Fill a gallon jug with 20 grams of wormwood, plus the hyssop, calamus, anise seed, fennel seed, star anise, coriander seed, and 6 grams of melissa. Add the moonshine, and soak for 1 week. Then add about ¼ gallon (1 L) of water, and soak for another few days.

Distill, discarding the heads and tails. (Heads are complete when the distillate begins to smell less bitter; tails begins when it starts to smell bitter again.) Distilling cuts the majority of the wormwood bitterness (supposedly the second-most bitter substance on earth), but leaves its medicinal properties. Some absinthes, especially Swiss ones, are served clear, but the famous green tint comes from a secondary maceration, which also serves to reintroduce more subtle flavors that were removed in the distillation. Combine your spirit with the mint, citron peel, licorice root, lavender, and ginger, as well as the remaining 2 grams of wormwood and 1.1 grams of melissa. Soak for 1 to 3 days, tasting twice a day. Strain when it reaches your preferred bitterness and sufficiently vibrant hue. Because of the natural sweetness of the moonshine, you will not need to sweeten the absinthe with a sugar cube in your glass. But you will definitely want to water it down. A ratio of 1 part absinthe, 6 parts ice-cold water is a heavenly summer-day drink.

TOBACCO BITTERS

BY CHRIS BEAR, MUSICIAN

The more I got interested in making cocktails, the more curious I got about bitters. They are a recurring theme in classic recipes, and an essential step in tying a drink together. But what are they? Angostura is a secretive company that does not disclose its recipe. But others have guessed at it, and soon I was deep in online forums, learning other people's methods and suggestions for ingredients.

One of the difficulties of making bitters is finding a place to buy the weird roots and herbs. In New York, there's a store in the East Village called Flower Power, run by hippie-ish women who call themselves green witches. They were mildly confused by what I was purchasing, since they mostly sell to people making teas or tinctures, but bitters are similarly medicinal—they just also involve alcohol.

Despite my attempt at making my batches small, I soon realized that it'd take me forever to go through them using a few drops at a time, so I started giving them out as gifts. I came up with a handful of flavors and packaged them together in small droppers along with labels suggesting cocktail recipes—I called them Bear's Bitters. From there, it's just been a process of trying different things out, throwing ingredients together, seeing what happens. I'm in a band that travels often, and I like to bring my bitters on the road with us. They were initially intended to spruce up whatever alcohol the venue provided for us, but given the amount of seltzer water we pillage on a daily basis, it didn't take long to discover that bitters also make for a crisp midday refreshment.

I first made my bitters with grain alcohol, but when Kings County opened, I started playing with their moonshine as the base spirit. This led me to stronger flavor profiles, since bitters is always going to have some flavor from the spirit you begin with. This one plays off of the old tradition of having a glass of whiskey and a cigarette. I thought about the natural elements of tobacco, which, in its raw, unsmoked state, can be a very fruity crop. It seemed like it would pair nicely with the corn whiskey.

RECIPE:

tobacco and wrapping
    from 1 cigar
1 tablespoon natural rolling
    tobacco
1 teaspoon Oregon grape
1 teaspoon black
    peppercorns
1 teaspoon allspice
½ teaspoon sassafras
1½ cups (360 ml) unaged
    whiskey

¼ teaspoon burdock
¼ teaspoon gentian
¼ teaspoon wormwood
½ teaspoon barberry
2 bags Lapsang souchong
    tea
1 cup (240 ml) water
¾ cup (165 g) light brown
    sugar

In a jar, combine the tobacco, Oregon grape, black peppercorns, allspice, and sassafras with the whiskey. Macerate for 2 weeks, shaking twice daily. Add the burdock, gentian, wormwood, barberry, and Lapsang souchong, and allow to macerate for another 2 weeks, shaking twice daily. Strain out the liquid and save the solid ingredients. Set aside the infused alcohol.

Add the solid ingredients to the water and bring to a boil. Allow to cool and pour back into a jar. Macerate the water mixture for 2 weeks, shaking twice daily. Strain out the liquid and discard the solid ingredients.

Combine the alcohol mixture and the water mixture. In a pan, caramelize the brown sugar and add to the liquid. Stir until the sugar dissolves. Allow to rest for 2 days. Strain through a very fine sieve a couple times until there is minimal sediment. Bottle.

BOURBON-SOAKED MAPLE SYRUP AND PANCAKES

BY EVEN HANZCOR, CHEF AND OWNER, PARISH HALL

When I think of great breakfasts, my mind goes to waffles and pancakes at home, the waffle flipping straight from the iron to the plate, smothered in syrup. And when I think of syrup, I think of fall walks on the roads around town in Redding, Connecticut. Though the maple runs in the spring, fall always seems more syrup's season—cool and heavy and dark, the air thick with chimney smoke.

Aging syrup in bourbon barrels is not a stunning idea, it just seems to make sense. There's a similar sweetness, the charred accents of the barrel, the symmetry of returning syrup to wood. So I showed up at Kings County one day, asking if we could experiment with a couple spent barrels, and we've been using them ever since, aging new batches as we go and using the syrupy empties for cocktails or vinegar.

At Parish Hall, we serve our syrup with johnnycakes and French toast, but it's amazing in a fall cocktail, as a glaze for pork or quail, drizzled over or churned into ice cream, or pretty much anything else.

RECIPE:

For the johnnycakes:

8 tablespoons (112 g) unsalted butter

2 tablespoons turbinado sugar

4 cups (600 g) stone ground cornmeal

2 teaspoons salt

2 cups (480 ml) whole milk

⅓ cup (75 ml) boiling water

For the syrup:

one 5-gallon (19-L) spent bourbon barrel

5 gallons (19 L) darkest grade-B maple syrup

Make the johnnycakes:
Cream the butter and sugar together in the mixer. Add
the cornmeal and salt and beat 1 minute, until light.
Add the milk, then add the boiling water to make a
moist but cohesive batter. You may need more water to
thin to the proper consistency. The batter will thicken as
it sits, so if you make it for later use, just thin with water
as needed before cooking.

Drop by large spoonfuls onto a hot greased griddle and
flatten slightly with the back of a spoon. Brown nicely,
turn, and cook through on the other side.

Make the syrup:
After discharging the bourbon from the barrel, return
the bung to the bunghole and wrap the barrel in plastic
wrap. This will ensure it retains as much bourbon flavor
as possible. When you are ready to add the syrup, do not
rinse the barrel with water. Just fill it with syrup. Store in a
refrigerator (you'll need a large one) or a consistently cool
place for 1 to 3 months, or longer. You may use the syrup at
any time and top off with new syrup, or simply siphon out
the syrup until the barrel is empty, then use the barrel for
something else. It's difficult to go wrong.

BOURBON SHRIMP
AND GRITS

BY JULIA ZEIGLER-HAYNES,
CHEF AND HOST OF THE DINNER BELL

Sometimes cooking with spirits is necessary to make the recipe work, and other times it's just the best use of the last sips of your bottle, when you don't have quite enough for two cocktails. Consider this recipe the latter, as well as a sly way of sneaking booze into your day before noon. It makes for a great brunch (try adding thick-cut bacon lardons or topping with a fried egg). But really, shrimp and grits can be devoured at any meal, paired with a slice of grilled bread and a bitter lettuce salad simply dressed with lemon and olive oil. Whatever you do, use domestic shrimp. Overseas farming of shrimp is a sketchy scene. Google "shrimp farming" if you are feeling bold . . . but don't say I didn't warn you.

RECIPE:

For the shrimp stock:
20 shrimp with shells on
1 tablespoon vegetable oil
2 cloves garlic, crushed
2 bay leaves
½ teaspoon black peppercorns
½ teaspoon fennel seed
1 pinch red chili flakes
5 cups (1.2 L) water

For the grits:
1 cup (242 g) grits (soaked
    overnight)
4 tablespoons (56 g) butter
1 cup (100 g) grated cheddar
    cheese

For the shrimp:
7 tablespoons (98 g) butter
1 large shallot, diced
3 cloves garlic, finely chopped
1 small bunch tarragon,
    stemmed and chopped
2 sticks celery, sliced thin
1 jalapeño, seeded and diced
juice of half a lemon
salt and pepper
3 ounces (90 ml) Kings County
    Bourbon
½ cup (15 g) flat-leaf parsley,
    loosely chopped
2 tablespoons chopped chives,
    for garnish

To get your stock going, first rinse and peel the shrimp, setting the shells aside. In a saucepan over medium heat, pour a tablespoon of vegetable oil and toss in the shrimp shells, stirring as they turn pink. Add the garlic and dry spices, sauté for 2 minutes, and then add the water. Turn the heat up to high, bring to a boil, and then lower heat to a lively simmer. Cook uncovered for 1 hour, ladling off any foamy bits that rise to the top. Strain the stock and discard the shells and spices. Return the stock to the saucepan and heat on high to reduce the liquid to 2 cups (480 ml).

The hearty, knobby grits popping up on menus these days (Anson Mills is a great purveyor) require a bit of a time commitment but are well worth the extra effort. To make the grits, follow the soaking/cooking directions that come with the grits you choose. Once cooked, add the butter and cheddar cheese shortly before serving, stirring to melt. Check the seasoning of the grits; add salt and pepper to taste.

To prepare the shrimp, in a heavy-bottomed saucepan, heat 3 tablespoons (42 g) of the butter over medium heat. Add the shallot and garlic, sauté until golden, and then add the tarragon, celery, jalapeño, and lemon juice. Let them sweat for 5 more minutes. Add the stock, and continue to cook over medium heat while you prepare the shrimp. Add salt and pepper to taste.

Melt the remaining 4 tablespoons (56 g) of butter in a skillet over medium-high heat. Pat the shrimp dry. When the butter begins to foam, add the shrimp in a single layer and cook until the bottom is opaque and pink; toss to flip the shrimp. Just before the shrimp are cooked through, add the whiskey. Flambé the shrimp, then combine with the shallot mixture. Heat together and stir to incorporate.

Spoon the grits into bowls and top with the shrimp and whiskey sauce. Garnish with parsley and chives. Serves 4 as a main course.

BOURBON CHOCOLATE CHIP COOKIES WITH TARRAGON AND BROWN BUTTER

BY ERIN PATINKIN AND AGATHA KUALAGA,
CO-FOUNDERS OF THE OVENLY BAKERY

Our first visit to Kings County was on an insufferably hot day. The distillery was located back then in a small corner of a converted warehouse in industrial Bushwick. There was no air conditioning. A shirtless and sweaty distiller was turning mash into liquor.

At that time, we had been experimenting with creating a bourbon cookie. So we took a few bottles home with us, and landed on one of our favorite recipes. Licorice and tarragon pair well with the sweetness of the bourbon, bitter chocolate enhances its caramel undertones, and nutty browned butter marries the flavors together.

RECIPE:

1 cup (230 g) butter

2½ cups (310 g) flour

¾ teaspoon baking soda

¾ teaspoon salt

1 cup (200 g) granulated sugar

¾ cup (165 g) light brown sugar

1 egg yolk

1 egg

1 teaspoon vanilla extract

¼ cup (60 ml) bourbon

1 cup (175 g) dark chocolate chips

1 tablespoon tarragon

In a saucepan over medium-low heat, melt the butter and continue to heat until it crackles and foams. Once the foam begins to subside, butter solids will quickly begin to brown on the bottom of the pan. At this point, stir continuously with a wooden spoon to scrape browned bits off the bottom of the saucepan. Once nutty brown in color, remove from the heat. Do not let the butter become black and burn. Set aside and let cool.

In a separate bowl, whisk together the flour, baking soda, and salt. Once the butter is at room temperature, add it to the bowl of a standing mixer. Add the sugar and brown sugar, and mix on medium until incorporated. Separate the yolk from the white of 1 egg and add it to a small bowl. Discard the white or save it for another use. Add the whole egg to the same bowl, and then, with the mixer on low, add slowly to the butter mixture. Raise the mixer to medium-high, and beat for 1 minute until smooth. Turn the mixer back to low, add the vanilla and bourbon, and beat until combined, about 30 seconds. Add the flour mixture and mix until barely incorporated, about 30 seconds. Then add the chocolate and tarragon, mixing until all the dry ingredients are incorporated, about 30 seconds more. Remove the bowl from the mixer, and chill for 30 minutes. Scoop with a small ice-cream scoop or form by hand into 1-inch (2.5-cm) balls onto parchment-lined sheet pans.

Preheat the oven to 350°F (175°C). Bake until light golden, about 10 minutes. Cookies will look slightly underbaked and soft in the center, but will set. Let cool before serving.

HILLBILLY BREAD

BY AN ANONYMOUS MOONSHINER
AND FRIEND OF THE DISTILLERY

When you move to New Hampshire, the first thing you want to do is get your name on the road-killed moose list down at the PD. That and the spring crop of fiddleheads assures you'll never go hungry. But the police offer no free moonshine. You'll be on your own there.

We tend to get everything we need in the Granite State (except dead moose) from the dump. I made my entire pot still from dump pickins, and to this day I get most of my fermentables from the dump's swap shop or the local thrift store. Some people get squeamish about cans of corn that are six years past expiration. Not me. I consider the whiskey it makes pre-aged. And I've found you can make great-tasting spirits from almost anything. The worse it tastes and smells going into the still, the better it seems to be coming out.

The best whiskey I ever made was from skunked beer. I found a couple of cases of very old home-brewed stout in Grolsch bottles at a yard sale. The thick black beer must have been ten years old and was obviously undrinkable, but I wanted the bottles. As I went to empty them out, I thought, "Why not?" and poured it directly into the still. It made the smoothest, hoppy all-barley whiskey without all the fuss of fermenting. Then I found a local store owner with a couple of cases of outdated Sam Adams that he was happy to see taken away. Perfect. Mellow, but with a hint of hoppiness. Now, if any of my friends have any beer grow old before they drink it, they know who to give it to.

The lesson is: Be resourceful. If it has starch, sugar, or alcohol in it, it is just whiskey in disguise. Unleash it. Set it free. Just don't get tricked into that "aging" thing. That's just a gimmick. Drink your shine right away, as it flows from the spout, before it even cools. Let the angels find their own share.

And also: Eat your mash!

RECIPE:

2 sticks (230 g) butter, at room temperature

3 cups (200 g) spent moonshine grains (don't rinse
    them or you'll wash out the yeast)

5 cups (625 g) all-purpose flour

1 cup (200 g) sugar

1 teaspoon salt

½ teaspoon grated lemon peel

1½ cups (360 ml) whole milk

1 cup (145 g) raisins (optional)

2 eggs

1 egg yolk (optional—for painting on the top of the
    dough before cooking)

Let the butter soften.

In a large bowl, mix together all the ingredients except the last egg yolk. You don't need any yeast—it's in the grains already.

Divide the dough and put it into two greased bread pans.

Put the pans into a warm place (about 85°F/29°C) for a few hours until the dough about doubles in size.

If desired, beat the egg yolk with a teaspoon or so of water, and paint this on the top of each loaf.

Bake at 350°F (175°C) for 45 minutes.

x x x

RESOURCES

If you are looking to go further into any of the topics presented in this book, I offer the following resources that might be of interest.

BOOKS ON AMERICAN WHISKEY

Bourbon, Straight: The Uncut and Unfiltered Story of American Whiskey by Chuck Cowdery.
A general overview of American whiskeys with some reviews.

Kentucky Bourbon Whiskey: An American Heritage by Michael R. Veach.
A great history that is derived from Veach's access to the United Distillers and Filson Club archives.

Chasing the White Dog by Max Watman.
A memoir about the writer's interest in home distilling and rural moonshining in his native Virginia.

TOURS

If you want to visit American whiskey distilleries, start in Kentucky with the Kentucky Bourbon Trail:
www.kybourbontrail.com

And then the Kentucky Bourbon Craft Trail:
www.kybourbontrail.com/craft-tour/

And while it's not on the Bourbon Trail, Buffalo Trace Distillery is worth a visit and has a great website:
www.buffalotracedistillery.com

Most craft distilleries offer tours, too. Kings County Distillery offers Saturday tours of its home at the Paymaster Building of the Brooklyn Navy Yard:
www.kingscountydistillery.com

A handful of other New York distilleries also offer tours; you can make an afternoon out of it.

If you are outside of Kentucky or New York, you're likely still close to a microdistillery. Find the one nearest you here:
www.distilling.com/DistilleryMap.html
But call ahead as this map can go out of date quickly.

AMERICAN WHISKEY BLOGS

The following are essential reading to stay up on whiskey news and to get informed, opinionated tastings:

The Chuck Cowdery Blog (chuckcowdery.blogspot.com)
Mash Notes (clayrisen.com)
Sku's Recent Eats (recenteats.blogspot.com)

BOOKS AND INFORMATION ON HOME DISTILLING

Making Pure Corn Whiskey: A Professional Guide for Amateur- and Micro-Distillers by Ian Smiley.
The definitive book for the home distiller, much more detailed than this book. Ignore the section about building a still and focus on the process.

Moonshine by Matthew B. Rowley.
Looks like a children's book, but actually has some useful information that is presented more clearly than in many other books.

Alt Whiskeys: Alternative Whiskey Recipes and Distillery Techniques for the Adventurous Craft Distiller by Darek Bell of Corsair Artisan Distillery.
A series of recipes using unusual grains for unconventional whiskeys.

Craft of Whiskey Distilling by Bill Owens / American Distilling Institute.
Focused on commercial distilling, but relevant to the home distiller.

Whisky: Technology, Production and Marketing (Handbook of Alcoholic Beverages), edited by Inge Russel.
A Scotch whisky classroom textbook, full of helpful information.

This forum is occasionally useful:
homedistiller.org

The following online shops sell home stills, yeast, grains, testing equipment, heat sources, pumps, and other supplies. Note that if you buy a still, these manufacturers are legally obliged to furnish the federal government with a list of their customers.
Brewhaus: www.brewhaus.com
Hillbilly Stills: www.hillbillystills.com
Mile Hi Distilling: www.milehidistilling.com

The Hydrometer Correction Table can be found here:
www.ttb.gov/foia/Gauging_Manual_Tables/Table_1.pdf

If you are interested in starting your own distillery, the American Distilling Institute offers resources for startup distillers:
www.distilling.com

The federal government will also guide you through certain requirements and has a helpful FAQ on the TTB page:
http://www.ttb.gov/nu/index.shtml

And finally, for a great book of whiskey recipes, for food and drink, get:
The Kentucky Bourbon Cookbook by Albert W. A. Schmid.
It features amazing recipes, including something described as "Jellied Kentucky Bourbon." Yes.

GLOSSARY

alcohol by volume – A measure of a spirit's alcohol content, this merely refers to the percent alcohol in a given sample. The standard baseline for most spirits is 40 percent alcohol, which means there is 40 percent ethanol and 60 percent water in a given spirit. Not to be confused with proof, which is measured in degrees, but is simply double the percent alcohol. A spirit that is 40 percent alcohol (or 40 percent abv) is also 80 proof or 80 degrees of proof. Proof is considered archaic, though the government still relies on it in written laws.

alembic still – See *pot still.*

barrel – A cylindrical wooden vessel for storing whiskey, often charred or toasted on the inside to promote interaction between the spirit it contains and the organic compounds in the wood. Called a "cask" in regard to Scotch whiskies.

beer – Another word for fermented mash or wash.

bottled in bond – A designation for straight whiskeys that are aged at least four years at a single distillery, and bottled at 100 proof. Distillers in the late 1800s fought hard for this designation to distinguish well-made whiskey from cheap imitation whiskey created by blending neutral spirit with flavorings and additives.

bourbon – Bourbon is a type of whiskey made from a mash of at least 51 percent corn; distilled at less than 160 proof; entered in charred, previously unused (new) oak barrels at 125 proof or less; and bottled at greater than 80 proof. This type of spirit, while mostly made in Kentucky, can be made anywhere in the United States.

column still – A type of still invented in the early 1800s that performs multiple distillations within the still itself, adding to greater efficiency and a more neutral spirit. Often, a column still is also a continuous or Coffey still, which allows for mash to be continually pumped through the still. Continuous distillation is distinct from batch distillation, where mash is fed into the still in batches.

condenser – A part of any still apparatus that uses a heat exchanger to condense vapor back to liquid. Often the cooling source is cold water.

corn whiskey – A type of American whiskey, distilled from a mash of 80 percent or more corn to less than 160 proof, and not necessarily exposed to charred wood. May be clear if unaged or lightly aged, or yellow if stored, aged, or rested in used or uncharred barrels.

distillery – A place where distilled spirits are made. Often confused with a brewery, which is where beer is made.

DSP – A federal designation for a distilled spirits plant, or a licensed distillery. All legal distilleries are assigned a DSP number. A DSP must abide by rules governing storage, accounting, and taxing of spirits.

ethanol – A common alcohol molecule, the one that we drink and are most familiar with. Also the type of alcohol that can be used as a substitute for gasoline.

feints – Any alcohol that is made during the spirit run that is rejected by the distiller and used to charge future runs of the still. Most often the heads and tails of any given run. In Scotland, the feints are just the tails.

fermentation – An organic process by which yeast converts sugars to alcohol. Used in the making of beer, wine, mead, and distilled spirits. Yeast consumes oxygen and sugar, and produces carbon dioxide and ethanol.

foreshots – The first drops of alcohol to come from a still. Alcohol boils at 173°F, but some trace organic compounds, such as acetone and methanol, boil at an even lower temperature. So the first drops of liquid off the still will contain a higher concentration of these lower-boiling-point compounds, which are toxic. Distillers collect these compounds and remove them from the production; they are used for cleaning or, as one distiller has pointed out, as "a great ant-killer."

heads – The first part of the spirit run, before the hearts. Heads are too volatile to drink, but close enough to the hearts that they get recycled into other batches. Heads immediately follow the foreshots. (This nomenclature is slightly different in Scotland, so beware the international nature of online forums.)

hearts – The middle of the spirit run, following the heads and preceding the tails. This is the mellowest, cleanest part of the whiskey run, usually occurring from 80 percent abv down to about 65 percent abv. It will subsequently be diluted to become your finished whiskey.

hybrid still – A still that is capable of distilling either as a column still or, if the column is bypassed, a pot still.

Lincoln County Process – Refers to filtering freshly distilled spirit through maple charcoal before entering the spirit into the barrel. Commonly associated with Tennessee whiskey. Jack Daniel's, the largest distillery to use this process and its inventor, was once located in Lincoln County, but as of this writing, there are no active distilleries in Lincoln County. State law now mandates the Lincoln County Process for any whiskey made in the state and named "Tennessee Whiskey."

low wines – In traditional whiskey distillation, whiskey is distilled twice to achieve a level of purity that is acceptable for consumption. Low wines are the cloudy, odorous spirits that are the result of the first distillation, usually of a lower proof and with more congeners than other alcohols.

malt – Malt refers to cereal grain seeds that have been allowed to begin the process of germination, but whose sprouting has been arrested just before shoots appear. Malted grains have a different enzyme composition from dormant grains, and these enzymes are what brewers and distillers use to convert the starch in grain to sugar. Malt powder, used in milkshakes and candies, is derived from this type of grain, and was considered a nutritional supplement in the late 1800s.

malt whiskey – In the United States, malt whiskey is any whiskey distilled from a mash bill of 51 percent or more of malted barley. Not to be confused with single malt whisky, which is a category of scotch. American malt whiskey must meet the other legal requirements for the "named" categories of American whiskey regarding distillation proof, barrel-entry proof, type of cooperage, and bottle strength.

mash – A thick grain porridge to which yeast is added before fermentation; it's the starting point of all whiskey. Some distillers call this "wash," which is any fermentable, sugar-rich liquid.

mash bill – The proportion of grains used in a given whiskey recipe.

moonshine – Moonshine generally refers to any illegally made spirit, but in the United States, this spirit was historically an unaged whiskey distilled from corn, usually bottled at a high proof in unmarked containers. Today, moonshine is considered a "fanciful" term by the government body that oversees the labeling of alcoholic beverages, and has no specific requirements. Any spirit today may be called moonshine, but it is used here as a synonym for unaged whiskey, though illegal Appalachian moonshine is often made with sugar (for the yeast) and corn (for flavor).

neutral spirit – Column-distilled spirit that exits the distillation process at close to 100 percent pure ethanol. Also known as GNS (grain neutral spirit) or NGS (neutral grain spirit), this is the base of many common spirits such as gin, absinthe, and vodka. Can be made with any source of sugar, but is most commonly made with grain (as with GNS or NGS). In Scotland, this type of spirit, if made from grain, is called grain whisky, but it would not meet the American definition of whiskey.

new make – Refers to undiluted clear spirit fresh from the still. Sometimes used interchangeably with "white dog" or "white whiskey," but the latter more commonly refers to diluted, finished spirit.

pot still – A traditional, crude type of still that consists of a kettle, a hollow neck, and a condenser. Compared to a column still, this type of still makes more flavorful, richer spirit that contains more impurities from its source. Also known as an alembic still.

proof – A measure of the alcoholic content of distilled spirits, proof is always twice the percent alcohol; i.e. a whiskey that is bottled at 40 percent alcohol by volume is also considered 80 proof. Since spirits are taxed by how much alcohol they contain, the accuracy of this number has been of great interest to the federal government over the years. According to some historians, the etymology of the word referred to the strength at which gunpowder soaked with a given spirit would still ignite; this process was called "proving a spirit" in order to ensure that it was not diluted before sale. Nearly all spirits are diluted with water to 80–100 proof after they are collected from the still, and in most cases are regulated by government code.

proof gallon – A unit of measure. Since spirit at a distillery is often distilled, stored, and bottled at different strengths, proof gallons are a consistent measure, defined as a gallon of spirit at 100 percent proof or 50 percent alcohol. A gallon of freshly distilled spirit at 75 percent alcohol is 1.5 proof gallons. A gallon of whiskey at 40 percent alcohol is .8 proof gallons.

reflux – The repeated conversion of a liquid to vapor and back within a still apparatus. Reflux results in a more neutral spirit as it removes impurities from the spirit. Many stills are designed to encourage reflux by mechanical means, either chilling the vapor in the column, forcing vapor through pools of liquid, or creating a large amount of surface area through column packing that enables a large surface area for condensation.

reflux still – See *column still*.

rye whiskey – A type of whiskey made from a mash of at least 50 percent rye, distilled at less than 160 proof, entered in charred, previously unused (new) oak barrels at 125 proof or less, and bottled at greater than 80 proof.

single malt whisky – In Scotch whisky, *single malt* is a protected designation for whiskey made at a "single" distillery from a mash bill of exclusively malted barley.

sour mash – A process wherein the spent distillate (the leftover mash in the still after a distillation run) is added to new mash, which lowers the pH and creates a more favorable environment for the yeast. This is similar in principle to sourdough starter. The alternative is a sweet mash process, in which whiskey is mashed independently of liquid from previous batches.

still – A device for separating and purifying alcohol from water by boiling. Since alcohol has a lower boiling point than water, boiling a mixture containing the two will crudely separate the alcohol from the water, reducing it to a purer form, or distilling it. A still is any device designed to vaporize a liquid and then condense the vapor back to liquid. An alcohol still consists of a heat source, a kettle, a vapor column, and a condenser cooled by cold water.

tails – The pungent, estery late part of a distillation run on a pot still. Commonly recycled into future runs.

Tennessee whiskey – Whiskey made in Tennessee. The term most often, but not always, describes whiskey that has been subjected to the "Lincoln County Process." Generally, Tennessee whiskey also meets the criteria to be called bourbon, but producers choose the narrower distinction of Tennessee whiskey.

TTB – The Alcohol and Tobacco Tax and Trade Bureau is an agency within the government formerly known as the ATF, but which was spun off during governmental reorganization after the Department of Homeland Security was created. The agency regulates the production, labeling, and taxation of alcoholic beverages under the Department of the Treasury. This branch is now distinct from the Bureau of Alcohol, Tobacco, Firearms and Explosives, which enforces laws relating to the illegal trafficking of these regulated items.

wash – Another word for mash, but commonly refers to mash that has had its solids removed.

whiskey – A distilled spirit made from grain, which is also defined by the proof at which it emerges from the still; for American whiskey, it must be below 160 proof. This refers to a cruder distillation process by which the spirit retains many of the compounds and flavors from the fermented mash. Vodka or neutral spirits can also be made from grain, but being distilled on more sophisticated equipment, they are able to redistill the spirit many times over in the still itself. Bourbon, rye, and scotch are all types of whiskey. Since most whiskey is aged in charred or toasted barrels, it's usually amber or brown in color, though some unaged whiskeys are clear.

white whiskey – Any unaged, clear whiskey.

worm – In distilling, the worm is a copper coil immersed in cold water that facilitates the condensation of alcohol vapor back to liquid ethanol. In most contemporary home stills, this is replaced with a shell-and-tube condenser.

Below are the common congeners that are present in distillation.

Acetaldehyde – Frequently blamed for hangover symptoms. Occurs also in tobacco and marijuana smoke. Irritates skin, eyes, nose, and throat. Can cause nausea, drowsiness, hallucinations, kidney and liver damage, respiratory paralysis, and death. Boiling point: 68°F (20°C).

Acetone – Commonly used as a solvent. It is a main ingredient in nail-polish removers and has medical uses in dermatology as chemical peels and acne medication. Health hazards are slight, as acetone occurs naturally in the body. Also used as a paint thinner. Boiling point: 133°F (56°C).

Ethyl Acetate – The ester of ethanol (booze) and acetic acid (vinegar). Used as a solvent and cleaning solution, and used to decaffeinate coffee and tea. Commonly considered a wine fault in young wines, it can dissipate through systemic aging (as with whiskey). Nontoxic. Boiling point: 171°F (77°C).

Methanol – Otherwise known as wood alcohol, methanol is the simplest of all alcohol molecules. Not to be confused with ethanol, which is the good stuff, it is an ingredient in the production of formaldehyde. Used commonly to "denature" alcohol, it makes drinking ethanol poisonous. Some bootleggers in Prohibition tried to separate the two by distillation with disastrous effects. Highly toxic, it forms formic acid, which can destroy the optic nerve (blinding the victim), and can cause headache, dizziness, confusion, lack of coordination, unconsciousness, and death. Doses as small as 10 ml can cause permanent harm, though home distillate is between .295 and .82 ml per drink, which is similar to or better than commercial whiskey and vodka. Boiling point: 148°F (64°C).

Propanol – Similar in effect and toxicity to alcohol, but two to four times more potent. Boiling point: 206–7°F (96–97°C).

Amyl Alcohol – Refers to any of eight alcohols with the formula $C_5H_{11}OH$, commonly called fusel alcohols (or erroneous fusel oils). Generally associated with the "tail" of the run—and esters can smell like banana, apricot, etc. Boiling point: varies.

Isopropyl Alcohol – Commonly used in medical applications like sterilizing pads and hand sanitizers. Many industrial uses as solvents and electronics cleaners. Symptoms of ingestion include flushing, headache, dizziness, nausea, vomiting, and coma. Unlike alcohol, can be toxic through absorption. Boiling point: 181°F (83°C).

Butanol – Refers to any of four higher-chain alcohols also in the "fusel oil" category of congeners in the "tail" of the run. Used in hydraulics, solvents, and perfumes. Considered toxic for consumption and a skin and eye irritant. Isobutanol is the most common butanol in whiskey and is less toxic than other butanols. Boiling point: varies.

Page numbers in *italics* refer to illustrations

A

absinthes, 26, *31*, 41–43, 105, 193–95

aging spirits, 24–25, 30, *30*, 54, 109–10, 144–46

Alcohol and Tobacco Tax and Trade Bureau [TTB], 96

alembic stills. *See* pot stills

Alltech (distillery), 99

American Distilling Institute, 13

American whiskeys, 25, *31*, 71, *72–73*
  branding and sourcing of, 110
  distinction from Scotch whiskeys, 107, 109
  family tree of, *72–73*
  shortage, 110–11
  See also craft whiskeys; Kentucky whiskeys

Anchor Distilling Company, 71, 93

Appalachian moonshiners. *See* moonshiners

appellation d'origine contrôlée (AOC), 110

Astor Wines (liquor store), 95

Atkins, Andy, 19

Austin, Nicole, *27*

B

Bailey, Mag, 11, *12*, 13, 14

Balcones (distillery), 96

barley, *30*

barley malt, 21, 109, 126, 127

barley-based whiskeys, 94

barrels, for aging spirits, 22, 24, *27*, *30*, 42–43, 54–55, *55*, 75, 109, *144*

bars, 159-160, 161-63, 164-66, 167-69

Basic Corn Whiskey recipe, 127–132, 134–146

batch distilling, 109

Beam, Inc., 81–84
  See also Jim Beam distillery

Beam, Jim, 82

Beam, Joseph, 77

Bear, Chris, 196–97

beer, 22, 115

Bell, Amy and Darek, 96

Bernheim (wheat whiskey), 78

Bhakta, Raj, 102

Birnecker, Robert and Sonat, 97

blended whiskeys, 107–9

bootleggers, 9–10, 11, 13, 14, 62

Boston Molasses Flood of 1919, 35

Bottled-in-Bond Act of 1897, 55–56

bottling, 54–56, 151

Bourbon Chocolate Chip Cookies with Tarragon and Brown Butter, 202–3

Bourbon County, 20, 42–43, 61, 99–100

Bourbon Shrimp and Grits, 200–201

bourbons, 19, 20, 21–22, 25, 71, 74, 79, 80, 82, 83–84, 86–87, 88, 89, 93, 95, 98, 99
  recipes and, 147, 198–99, 200–201, 202–3

Bourbon-Soaked Maple Syrup and Pancakes, 198–99

branding. *See* labeling

brandy, 21, 24, 27, *31*, 35, 149

Breaking & Entering (bourbon), 93

Brewer's Whiskey, 97

Brewhaus, 120, 133

brewing, home, 21, 115

Bridges, John, 53

Brooklyn, New York, 14–15, 61–62, 63, *64–65*
  history of distilling and, 36, 43, 47–48, 64–65
  raids of illicit moonshiners in, history of, 47–49, *50–51*, 52–54
  Spoelman's first time firing up a still, 118–19

Brooklyn Bridge, 63, *64*

Brooklyn Heights, 37, 62, 64

Brooklyn Navy Yard, 15, 47–48, 49, 53, 62

Brown, George Garvin, 54–55, 80

Brown-Forman distillery, 79–80

Brueckelen Distilling, 104

Buffalo Trace, 85–87, 110–11

Building 92, Brooklyn, 63, *65*

Bulleit Bourbon, 74, 89

Bulleit Rye, 89

Burks Spring Distillery, 84

Byrne, Mark, 192

C

Campfire (blend of bourbon, rye, and scotch), 101

Canadian whisky, 21, *31*

Capone, Al, 62, 102

Caribbean, *31*

Cassidy, Michael, 53

cattle, 46, *47*

Certificate of Label Approval (COLA), 151

Cherry Bounce recipe, 178–79

Civil War, the, 27, 28, 46, 47, 48

Clear Creek (distillery), 93

Coale, Ansley, 93

cocktails, 168–171

Coffey, Anneas, 22

collection-jar method, 139–141, 142

Colonel Vaughn Wilson, 120–21

column distillation, 22–23, *30*

column stills, 122

condensors, 122–23, 133, 134

continuous stills, 109

contract distillers, 101–2, 111

copper pot stills, *92*, 122

corn grown for whiskey, *20*, 21, 25, *30*, 90, 91

corn whiskey, 24, 78, 90, 91, 104
  of King's county Distillery, 124–132, 134–146

Corsair Artisan Distillery, 96, *97*

Cowdery, Chuck, 69, 76

craft distilleries, 13–14, 71, 76, 86, 91, 150–53, *154–55*

craft whiskeys, 90–106

Crooked Creek Corn (heirloom corn), 104

Crow, James, 83

Cumberland Gap, 41, *42*, 45

Cunningham & Harris Distillery, 63, *64*

cylinders, graduated, *123*

D

Dad's Hat distillery, 104

Davis, Bryan, 106

Death's Door (distillery), 94–95

Delaware Phoenix, 105

Derek (friend of Spoelman), 9

Diageo, London, England, 89

Dickson's Alley, 62, 63, *65*

Dickson's Alley raid, 48, 52

distillation
  column, reflux or fractional, 22–23, *30*
  high-proof, 22–23, 30, 109, 134, 135
  history of, 35, 36, 37, *38–39*, 40–43, *44–45*, 46–49, *50–51*, 52–56, *57*, 58–59, *60*, 61–62, 63, *64–65*
  low-proof, 22, 30, 109
  run, graph of, *139*

distilled beer, whiskey made from, 22

distilled spirits. *See* Statement of Distilled Spirits; *specific distilled spirits by name*

distilleries
  contract, 101–2, 111
  large, 75–76, 86, 92, 110

single, 109
small, 21–22, 110
starting, 150–53
See also craft distilleries; home distilleries; home distilling
Doan, Otis, 12
Dry Manhattan (Lerner), 58
DSP (Distilled Spirits Plant), 110

E
1869 moonshine raid, 47–49, *50–51*, *52–54*
El Charrito restaurant, 13
electricity, 117
Elford, Chris, 186–87
Elijah Craig (bourbon), 19, 74
Erenzo, Ralph, 91, 103
Estabrooke, Brad, 104
ethanol, distilled, 26
excise taxes, 46–48, 54, 58, 115–16
explosions, 117

F
family tree, American whiskeys, *72–73*
federal government. *See* government, federal
federal licensing. *See* licensing
fermented grain mash, 22, *23*, 25
See also mash bills
fermenting, 130
FEW Spirits, 104
Fifth Ward of Brooklyn, 47–49, *50–51*, *52–54*
fires, 117
flavorings, 30, *31*, 118–19
floor plans, craft distilleries, *154–55*
Flying Dog Brewery, 94
Four Roses distillery, 88, 89
42 Fuhrman Street, 63, 64
fractional distillation, 22–23
Frank Leslie's Illustrated Newspaper, *50–51*, 52
Frizell, St. John, 176–77
fruit
based distillation, 93
brandies, 95
for making spirits, *30*

G
Garden Cocktail recipe, 182–83
geography, 30, *31*, *44–45*
George Dickel whiskey, 89
George III, King, 37
Germain-Robin (distillery), 93
Germain-Robin, Hubert, 93
Gilbert, Clinton, 53

gin, 24, 26, 27, *31*
Gorman, John, 53
government, federal, 24
See also licensing; Prohibition; taxes
Graber, Jess, 94
graduated cylinders, *123*
grain whisky (Scotland), 23, *31*
grains for making spirits, *20*, 21, 22, 25, *30*, 43, 46, 69, 90, 91, 109, 125–26, 127–28
Grant, Ulysses S., 48, 56

H
Halstead, Brianna, 182–83
Hamilton, Alexander, 37, 40
hand-built stills, 106
Haney, Mike, 14
Hanzcor, Even, 198–99
Harlan, Kentucky, 9–14, *10*
Haskell, David, 14, 118, 174–75
Hayden, Basil, 83
heat sources, 120, 122, *133*
Heaven Hill distillery, 77–78, 111
heirloom corn whiskey, 90, 91, 104
High West Distillery, 101
high-proof distillation, 22–23, 30, 109, 134, 135
Hillbilly Bread, 204–5
Hillbilly Flute (moonshine still), 14
Hillbilly Stills, 14, 120, 133
history. *See* distillation, history of
Hollyman, Helen, 188–89
home bars, 159–169
home brewing, 21, 115
home distilleries, assembling
condensors, 122–23
heat sources, 122
hydrometers, 124
ingredients for, 124–26
safety and, 117
the still, 120–22, *133*
thermometers, 123
See also stills, making
home distilling, 20, 62, *133*
aging, 144–46
fermenting, 130
mashing, 127–29
other recipes, 147–49
proofing, 142–43
the spirit run, 137–141
starting a craft distillery and, 150–53
straining, 131
the stripping run, 132, 134
testing the proof, 134–36

home teams, craft whiskeys, 98–100
Horwich, Charlie, 190
House Spirits Distillery, 105
hubris, 118–19
Hudson Avenue, Vinegar Hill, 63, *65*
hydrometers, *123*, 124, 129, 135

I
illicit moonshiners, 115
See also moonshiners, raids on illicit
income related to spirits, 58
ingredients, *30*, 124–26
innovators, craft whiskeys, 96–97
insurances, 152
international whiskeys, 21, 25
See also specific types of international whiskeys by name
Ireland, *31*
Irish immigrants, 43, 46
Irish whiskeys, 21, 23, *31*
Irishtown, Brooklyn, 48–49, 52, 62
Islay, Scotland, 109

J
Jack Daniel's, 22, 24, 54–55, 61, 80, 108
Jacob's Ghost whiskey, 83
Jameson (whiskey), 23–24
Japan, *31*, 88
Japanese whiskey, 21, *31*
Jefferson, Thomas, 27, 41
Jim Beam, 61, 71, 74, *75*–76, 81
See also Jim Beam distillery
Jim Beam distillery, *70*, 81
See also Beam, Inc.
Jim Beam White Label, 81, 82
Johnson's (Brooklyn distillery), 46
Johnson's Distillery, 63, *64*
Jones, Paul Jr., 88

K
Kentucky, history of distilling, 35, *44–45*, 59, 61
See also Harlan, Kentucky
Kentucky Bourbon Barrel Ale, 99
Kentucky Bourbon Distillers, 98
Kentucky Bourbon Trail, 71
Kentucky bourbons, 22, 74, 98, 99
Kentucky whiskeys, 69, *70*, 71–88, 92
Kidde, Jeremy, 95
Kings County Distillery, 14–15, *24*, *27*, 48, 62, 63, *65*, *92*, 119, *150*
corn whiskey recipe, 124–132, 134–146
first legal whiskey of, *28*

licensing of, 151
Kinstlick, Michael, 13
Kirin (Japanese beverage company), 88
Koval (distillery), 97
Kualaga, Agatha, 202–3
Kulsveen, Janelle, 98

L
labeling, 24, 71, 75–76, 110, 152
*Last Call: The Rise and Fall of
Prohibition* (Okrent), 46
Lawrenceburg, Indiana, 69
laws
    governing scotch, 107, 110
    for making whiskey, 115–16
    for whiskey labels, 75
    See also licensing; Prohibition
LDI (Lawrenceburg Distillers Indiana),
    89, 101, 102
Lee, Brian, 91
Lerner, Michael, 58
Lexington, Kentucky, 45, 99
licensing, 47, 61, 90–91, 95, 115,
    150–52
Lincoln County Process, 22, 80
Lins, Cheryl, 105
Lion's Pride whiskeys, 97
liqueurs, 26
Little Street, Brooklyn, 63, 65
Livingston Distillery, 36, 37, 43
Livingston/Pierrepont Distillery, 62,
    63, 64
Lohman, Sarah, 178–79
Lost Spirits distillery, 105, 106
Louisville, Kentucky, 61, 77, 79–80
Low Gap Whiskey, 93
low-proof distillation, 22, 30, 109
Luce, Nate, 193–95
Lyons, Pearse, 99

M
Mag's. *See* Bailey, Mag
Maker's 46, 84
Maker's Mark, 84, 110
Maker's Mark distillery, 83–84
Making Pure Corn Whiskey (Smiley),
    125
malt whiskey, 21, 97, 148–49
malted barley, 21, 109, 126, 127
Manhattan recipe, 176–77
map of whiskey history, 44–45
marketing, 152
mash bills, 69, 71, 76, 80, 84, 86–87,
    88
    See also fermented grain mash
mashing, 127–29, 147

Maysville, Kentucky, 45, 61
MB Roland (distillery), 98
McMahon, James, 53
Meadow of Love (absinthe), 105–6
"medicinal" whiskey, 85
Mellow Corn whiskey, 78
mescal, 24, 27, 31
Metropolitan Magazine, 53
Mexico, 31
MGP (food conglomerate), 69
microdistilleries, 90–91
    See also craft distilleries
Mihalich, Herman, 104
Mile Hi Distilling, 120, 133
Mint Julep recipe, 172–73
Mississippi, 61
molasses, 30
Moody, Ken, 13
moonshine, 15, 25, 28, 148
moonshine raid of 1869, 47–49,
    50–51, 52–54
moonshiners, 13–14, 28, 53, 59
    Prohibition and, 61
    raids on illicit, history of, 47–49,
    50–51, 52–54
Moor, Robert, 180–81
Morgan, John Pierpont, 43
Morris, Chris, 80, 121–22
Mount Vernon, 103
Muldoon, Dennis, 52

N
Nascar Fizz recipe, 186–87
neutral grain spirit (NGS), 23
neutral spirits, 30, 31
New Amsterdam, 35
New Holland Brewery and Distillery,
    96–97
New Orleans, 41–42
New Orleans Sno-Ball Julep recipe,
    188–89
New York, 43, 46
    history of distilling and, 35, 37
    microdistillery licenses, 90–91
    See also Brooklyn, New York
New York City, 15
New York Times, 49, 52
92 Navy Street, 63, 65
Noe, Booker, 82
Noe, Fred, 82
Number 12 whiskey, 89

O
Okrent, Daniel, 46
Old Crow whiskey, 83
Old Fashioned recipe, 174–75

Old Forester bourbon, 80
Old Grand-Dad whiskey, 82–83
Old Pogue (distillery), 99–100
Old Potrero (distillery), 71
Old Potrero Whiskey, 93
Old Scout (sourced whiskey line), 102
Old Tub whiskey, 83
    See also Jim Beam
organic farms and ingredients, 97,
    100, 102, 125
Oscar Pepper Distillery, 83
outliers, craft whiskeys, 105–6

P
packaging, 152
Pappy Van Winkle bourbon, 87
Parish Hall, 198–99
Pataki, George, 91
Patinkin, Erin, 202–3
Paymaster Building, Brooklyn Navy
    Yard, 15
peat fires, 109
Pennsylvania, 40, 45
percent proof. *See* proofing
Perfect Manhattan recipe, 190
Pickerell, Dave, 102
Pierrepont, Hezekiah, 43
Pine Mountain bootlegger, 9, 11
pioneers, craft whiskeys, 93–95
Pleasanton, Alfred, 48–49
Pogue House, 99
pot distillation, 30
pot stills, 22, 23, 30
    at Kings County Distillery, 24, 92
    for making whiskey, 120, 121–22,
    132
    safety regarding, 117
    single malt scotch and, 109
Presbyterian recipe, 191
profits, 58
Prohibition, 9, 13, 27–28, 46, 58–59,
    61, 85, 102
    See also bootleggers
prohibition on home distillation,
    115–16
proofing, 124, 135, 140, 141, 142–43
Purviance, Samuel, 43

R
Radcliffe, John, 90–91
raids, illicit moonshiners, 47–49,
    50–51, 52–54
Ratzer Map of Brooklyn, The, 36
recipes, 172–205
    home distilling, 147–49

of King's county Distillery corn
whiskey, 124–132, 134–146
See also specific recipes by name
reflux
distillation, 22–23
moonshine stills, 14
stills, 120–21
regulations. *See* licensing
Rendezvous Rye, Bourye, 101
rum, 21, 24, 27, *31*, 35, 37
Rumble Seat recipe, 184–85
Rupf, Jörg, 93
rural distilling, 37, 40, 59
Russian Samovar restaurant, 26
rye grains, 21, 25, *30*, 43, 69
rye whiskey, 69, 71, 74, 101–2, 103, 104

S
safety, in assembling home distillery, 117
Samuels, Bill Sr., 84
Samuels, Margie, 84
Samuels, T. W., 83–84
Sands Street, 63, *64*
Sands Street Gate, 63, *65*
Sazerac, 85, 193
Schmitz, Angela, 191
Scotch whiskys, 21, 25, *31*, 107–11
Scotland, *31*, *75*, 90, 107–8, 109
Scotland, grain whisky, 23
Seagram's, 69, 71
77 whiskeys, 104
Shapira, Max and Andy, 77–78
Short Mountain (distillery), 100
shortage, American whiskeys, 110–11
single malt scotch, 107, 108–9, 110
single malt whiskey recipe, 148–49
Sitzel-Weller Distillery, 61
small batch, 91
Smiley, Ian, 125
Smitty (friend of Spoelman), 11–12
Smooth Ambler, 102
sour mash recipe, 147
sourcers, craft whiskeys, 101–2
Spain, *31*
speakeasies, 59
spirit run, *136*, 137–141, *139*
Spoelman, Colin, 9–15, 19–21, *142*
bar of, 161–63
first time firing up a still, 118
Mint Julep recipe, 172–73
Squibb Distillery, 69
St. George (distillery), 93, *94*
Statement of Distilled Spirits, *60*
Staten Island, New York, 35

stills, making, 14, 106, 115
and assembling or purchasing, 120–24, *133*
hubris and, 118–19
licensing, 115
safety in assembling, 117
See also pot stills
Storm King Distillery, 90
straining, 131
Stranahan, George, 94
Strathisla distillery, *108*
stripping run, 132, 134–36
sugarcane, *30*
sugar-wash moonshine recipe, 148

T
Tate, Chip, 96
taxes
history of distilling and, 37, 40, 46–48, 56, 58
making whiskey and, 115–16
Templeton (rye whiskey), 101–2
Tennessee whiskeys, 22, 45, 80, 89
testing the proof, 134–36
thermometers, 123, *133*
Thompson, Hunter S., 94
Tobacco Bitters recipe, 196–97
Toddies, Hot and Cold, 180–81
Tomaszewski, Mary Beth and Paul, 98
Torgersen, John, 90–91
Town Branch (distillery), 99
toxicity, 117, 132
traditionalists, craft whiskeys, 103–4
Troy & Sons distillery, 104
TTB, 150
Tuthilltown Spirits distillery, 103–4

unaged spirits, 24–25, 30, *30*, 54, 61
United States, *31*
urban distilling, history of, 35, 43, 46
See also craft distilleries;
distillation, history of;
distilleries

U
U.S.S. *Catalpa*, 49

V
Veach, Michael, 69
Vendome, 98
ventilation, for stills, 117
Very Old Scout (sourced whiskey line), 102
Virginia, 45
vodka, 23, 24, 25–27, *31*, 121
Volstead Act, 58

W
W. L. Weller wheated bourbon, 87
Walker, Alexander, 108
Walker, John, 107–8
Walton Waters (absinthe), 105–6
Warwick Valley (distillery), 95
Washington, George, 27, 41, 46, 103
Washington's Rye Whiskey, 103
Webber, Andrew, 96
Western Sizzlin,' 13
wheat, *30*
wheat bourbons, 84
wheat whiskeys, 78, 94–95
Wheatley, Harlan, 86
Whiskey Highball recipe, 192
Whiskey Rebellion, 40–41
Whiskey Ring scandal of 1875, 56
"whiskey wars, the," 47–49, *50–51*, 52–54
WhistlePig distillery, 71, 102
Willard, Frances Elizabeth (Catherine), 104
Willett Distillery, 98
Willey, Tristan, 184–85
wines, *31*, 115
Woodford Reserve, 74, *75*, 80, 121–22
Woodford Reserve bourbon, 79

Y
yeast, 126, 127, 129
YouTube videos, 14

Z
Zeigler-Haynes, Julia, 200–201
Zeppelin Bend malt whiskey, 97

David and Colin, 2010.

ABOUT THE AUTHORS

Kings County Distillery is New York City's oldest operating whiskey distillery, the first since the Prohibition era within the city limits. It was founded in 2010 in a one-room, 325-square-foot studio in East Williamsburg, where homemade moonshine and bourbon were produced on five 24-liter stainless-steel stills running whiskey seven days a week, 16 hours a day. In 2012, the distillery moved into the Paymaster Building in the historic Brooklyn Navy Yard, just steps from the site of the legendary Brooklyn Whiskey Wars of the late 1860s and the former distillery district on the waterfront. The distillery was built to exact specifications: its copper gooseneck whiskey stills were fabricated in Scotland; its wooden fermenters were built locally by the firm responsible for many of the rooftop water tanks around New York City. The distillery grows corn and barley at a small educational grain garden on site, and spent grain is recycled as compost and pig feed.

Kings County's whiskeys have won numerous medals at the American Distilling Institute's Craft Spirit Awards and have been praised in Jim Murray's *Whisky Bible* as "absolutely spot on," "sweet, clean" with "sumptuous texture," and "very well made," earning very high marks among peer whiskeys from distilleries large and small. The distillery is open for tours and tastings each Saturday afternoon, and was named one of the best craft distillery tours in the country by thedailymeal.com.

Colin Spoelman grew up in rural Kentucky, where he was first exposed to moonshine, bootleggers, and cheap bourbon. After moving to Brooklyn, he began to experiment with home distilling, starting with unaged corn whiskeys and moving to bourbon, gaining most of his expertise through simple trial and error. He has worked in film, architecture, and perfume and operates as Kings County's Master Distiller. David Haskell grew up in New York City and Connecticut, and met Colin at Yale. After graduation, he received a Gates Scholarship to study architecture at Cambridge University, where he founded *Topic* magazine. He brought that magazine to New York, and spent a few years waiting tables while editing it. He is now Deputy Editor at *New York* magazine.

ACKNOWLEDGMENTS

We are grateful to a number of individuals who were instrumental to this book's publication. David Kuhn suggested we write it and, with Nicole Tourtelot, helped us realize it. Thank you to our editor, Deborah Aaronson, who immediately understood our sensibility and knew how to translate it on the page; Deb Wood, our very talented and patient designer; John Gall, who designed our cover; and everyone at Abrams who has been so supportive of this project. There were a few individuals who agreed to share their knowledge specifically for this book: Chris Morris at Woodford Reserve, Max Shapira at Heaven Hill, Mike Haney at Hillbilly Stills, Ralph Erenzo at Tuthilltown, Jeremy Kidde at Warwick Valley, and Julie Suarez at New York Farm Bureau. Sarah Lohman of fourpoundsflour.com has done research that provided the basis for the walking tour of Brooklyn's distilling history. And thanks, of course, to everyone who contributed recipes, and to Jonathan Wingo for his close read of the manuscript.

We also owe a great debt to everyone who has worked for the distillery; their ideas and dedication have contributed to the quality and character of our whiskeys, or at least our lives while making it. They are, in rough order of their tenure: Mark Byrne, Todd Kahler, Robert Moor, Nicole Austin, Matthew Million, Nate Luce, Paul Monnes, Anna Margaret and Helen Hollyman, Chris Elford, Tristan Willey, Simon Jolly, Christopher Harrington, Brianna Halstead, Greg Jeske, Charlie Horwich, Evan McCune, Ben Clements, Angie Schmitz, Rob Easter, Andrew Lohfeld, Jonathan Wingo, and Andy Lopez, as well as interns AJ Koger, Becca Goldstein, Will Schragis, John Seabrook, and Jordan Spitzer.

There are also a handful of people who have been especially supportive of our business: Doug Jaffe, Paul Sohn, Jesse Du Bey, and John Haskell; Andrew Kimball, Matt Hopkins, and Chris Tepper at the Brooklyn Navy Yard; the brothers Haslegrave; Phil Morgan at Hecho; John Bedard and Adam Kushner at Kushner Studios; Annie Novak and Emily Francois at Eagle Street Rooftop Farm; Laurent Danthine at Arcadian Pastures Farm; the folks at Lakeview Organic Grain, the Barrel Mill, and the Brooklyn Grange; Chris and Robert at Kings County Jerky for the moral support back at Meadow Street; and Leonard Fogelman, attorney at law, whose legal acumen is unmatched. And special thanks to Stefan Talman, who first suggested pot distillation instead of reflux, and whose early intuition in distilling helped teach Colin as a distiller.

We also want to thank the liquor stores, bars, and restaurants that have taken a chance on doing business with us—as well as our loyal customers, who have been enormously supportive from the day we opened.

And finally, thank you, Esteban and Ry, for your patience.

Editor: Deborah Aaronson
Designer: Deb Wood
Production Manager: Anet Sirna-Bruder

Library of Congress Control Number:
2013935900

ISBN: 978-1-4197-0990-6

Printed and bound in the United States
10 9

Abrams books are available at special discounts
when purchased in quantity for premiums and
promotions as well as fundraising or educational
use. Special editions can also be created to
specification. For details, contact specialsales@
abramsbooks.com or the address below.

The material contained in this book is presented
only for informational and artistic purposes.
The publisher and the author do not condone
or advocate in any way illegal activity of any
kind. If you engage in any of the activities
discussed in this book, you are doing so at
your own risk. The publisher and author accept
no responsibility for any liability, loss or risk,
personal or otherwise, which is incurred as a
consequence, directly or indirectly from the use
and application of any of the contents of this
publication.

PHOTO CREDITS

Ian Allen: p. 218; Liz Barclay: pp. 23, 153;
Daniel Bernauer: pp. 28, 136; © Bettmann/
CORBIS: pp. 50–51; Michael Bloom
Photography: p. 103; Chivas Brothers: p. 108;
Cornell University Political Americana
Collection, 1876: p. 56; Amy Davis: p. 144;
Rob Easter: p. 15; Filson Club Archives: p. 55;
Herald Post Collection, [ULPA 1994.18.0285],
1994.18, Photographic Archives, University
of Louisville, Louisville, Kentucky: p. 42;
Frank Leslie's Illustrated Newspaper Archives:
p. 47; Randy Harris: p. 100; David Haskell:
p. 150; High West Distillery & Saloon: p. 101;
Ben Krantz: p. 94; Anthony Matula: p. 97;
Metropolitan Magazine, 1909: p. 53; National
Photo Company Collection (Library of
Congress), Library of Congress Prints and
Photographs Division Washington, D.C. 20540:
p. 59; Picture Collection, The New York Public
Library, Astor, Lennox and Tilden Foundations:
p. 40; *Plan of the City of New York in North
America*. Bernard Ratzer. ca. 1770. nyc-1770.
fl.f.ra. Brooklyn Historical Society: p. 36;
John Pogue: p. 99; Valery Rizzo: pp. 20, 24, 27;
Ry Russo-Young: pp. 10, 12, 75, 77, 79, 121,
123, 140, 142; Colin Spoelman: pp. 70, 81, 85,
88, 92, 161, 164, 167; Taylor Strategy: p. 89;
Hannah Whitaker, *New York Magazine*: pp. 125,
128, 129, 130, 131, 132, 134, 135

ILLUSTRATION CREDITS

Heesang Lee: pp. 38–39, 44–45, 64–65, 133,
139, 154–55; Sebit Min: pp. 30–31, 72–73

THE ART OF BOOKS SINCE 1949

115 West 18th Street
New York, NY 10011
www.abramsbooks.com